I0417191

U.S. ELECTION SUPPORT IN AFRICA

HEARING

BEFORE THE

SUBCOMMITTEE ON AFRICA, GLOBAL HEALTH, GLOBAL HUMAN RIGHTS, AND INTERNATIONAL ORGANIZATIONS

OF THE

COMMITTEE ON FOREIGN AFFAIRS
HOUSE OF REPRESENTATIVES

ONE HUNDRED FOURTEENTH CONGRESS

FIRST SESSION

_____

MARCH 18, 2015

_____

Serial No. 114–19

_____

Printed for the use of the Committee on Foreign Affairs

Available via the World Wide Web: http://www.foreignaffairs.house.gov/ or http://www.gpo.gov/fdsys/

_____

U.S. GOVERNMENT PUBLISHING OFFICE

93–820PDF   WASHINGTON : 2015

_____

For sale by the Superintendent of Documents, U.S. Government Publishing Office
Internet: bookstore.gpo.gov   Phone: toll free (866) 512–1800; DC area (202) 512–1800
Fax: (202) 512–2104   Mail: Stop IDCC, Washington, DC 20402–0001

COMMITTEE ON FOREIGN AFFAIRS

EDWARD R. ROYCE, California, *Chairman*

CHRISTOPHER H. SMITH, New Jersey
ILEANA ROS-LEHTINEN, Florida
DANA ROHRABACHER, California
STEVE CHABOT, Ohio
JOE WILSON, South Carolina
MICHAEL T. McCAUL, Texas
TED POE, Texas
MATT SALMON, Arizona
DARRELL E. ISSA, California
TOM MARINO, Pennsylvania
JEFF DUNCAN, South Carolina
MO BROOKS, Alabama
PAUL COOK, California
RANDY K. WEBER SR., Texas
SCOTT PERRY, Pennsylvania
RON DeSANTIS, Florida
MARK MEADOWS, North Carolina
TED S. YOHO, Florida
CURT CLAWSON, Florida
SCOTT DesJARLAIS, Tennessee
REID J. RIBBLE, Wisconsin
DAVID A. TROTT, Michigan
LEE M. ZELDIN, New York
TOM EMMER, Minnesota

ELIOT L. ENGEL, New York
BRAD SHERMAN, California
GREGORY W. MEEKS, New York
ALBIO SIRES, New Jersey
GERALD E. CONNOLLY, Virginia
THEODORE E. DEUTCH, Florida
BRIAN HIGGINS, New York
KAREN BASS, California
WILLIAM KEATING, Massachusetts
DAVID CICILLINE, Rhode Island
ALAN GRAYSON, Florida
AMI BERA, California
ALAN S. LOWENTHAL, California
GRACE MENG, New York
LOIS FRANKEL, Florida
TULSI GABBARD, Hawaii
JOAQUIN CASTRO, Texas
ROBIN L. KELLY, Illinois
BRENDAN F. BOYLE, Pennsylvania

AMY PORTER, *Chief of Staff*   THOMAS SHEEHY, *Staff Director*

JASON STEINBAUM, *Democratic Staff Director*

————

SUBCOMMITTEE ON AFRICA, GLOBAL HEALTH, GLOBAL HUMAN RIGHTS, AND INTERNATIONAL ORGANIZATIONS

CHRISTOPHER H. SMITH, New Jersey, *Chairman*

MARK MEADOWS, North Carolina
CURT CLAWSON, Florida
SCOTT DesJARLAIS, Tennessee
TOM EMMER, Minnesota

KAREN BASS, California
DAVID CICILLINE, Rhode Island
AMI BERA, California

CONTENTS

U.S. ELECTION SUPPORT IN AFRICA

WEDNESDAY, MARCH 18, 2015

House of Representatives,
Subcommittee on Africa, Global Health,
Global Human Rights, and International Organizations,
Committee on Foreign Affairs,
Washington, DC.

The subcommittee met, pursuant to notice, at 10:15 a.m., in room 2255 Rayburn House Office Building, Hon. Tom Emmer (acting chairman of the subcommittee) presiding.

Mr. Emmer. Today's subject is U.S. election support in Africa. And I will recognize myself for an opening statement.

Good morning to all of you. I would like to thank our witnesses for coming before our subcommittee today to testify on U.S. election support in Africa. I specifically want to wish Chairman Smith, who is unable to be here today, well and please know he cares deeply about this issue in the African continent. Myself, along with Ranking Member Bass, will do our best in his absence. At this point I would ask that Chair Smith's remarks be entered into the record.

We will have two separate panels this morning to provide us with a better understanding of the shifting landscape on the African continent. The current situation is that Africa is complex with many African nations holding national elections this year while enduring ongoing political and civil instability. Many of the nations such as Nigeria, Central African Republic, and South Sudan are experiencing difficulties providing proper security in the face of grave threats such as Boko Haram, civil war, and regional tension.

In the face of these challenges, the United States is dealing with fiscal restraints that require us to make difficult choices. By prioritizing funds to high-risk states, we risk being late to the party.

I appreciate the opportunity to hear what we are doing to provide assistance and how we are coordinating with the U.N., NGOs, and the states themselves. Many nations, Nigeria, in particular, present many challenges as the current status of elections has been in great flux. I would particularly like to know today what the U.S. is doing to prepare for the elections now slated for March 28th. The vote may prove to be the most significant political event in Africa this year.

With over 10,000 people killed and millions displaced since 2009, the security situation is dire. The United States must provide leadership as Africa's largest economy hangs on by a thread. While there is great uncertainty in Africa, there are also real signs of

(1)

hope and progress. While many of these states are struggling to forge democratic regimes, they are at least transitioning to them. While our own fight for democracy was messy, this is to be expected.

The United States must continue to support these young nations as it is vital to our interests, regional security, and economic growth, and to the entire world as Africa continues to integrate itself into the global economy.

With that, I would like to yield to Ranking Member Bass for her opening statement.

Ms. BASS. Thank you very much, Mr. Chair. I want to thank Chairman Smith. I know he is not with us today. I heard he was under the weather, but I want to thank him even though he is not here for his leadership and for calling today's hearing and for you for serving in this capacity, to give us the opportunity to examine in depth, the U.S.'s approach and prioritization of not only our Government's direct election support, but also our wider democracy and governance efforts in support of processes that should take place before and after election events.

I would also like to thank our distinguished witnesses for today, as well as several Africa-focused and election experts from leading NGOs in the field of democracy and governance. I look forward to hearing your perspectives based on the areas of focus of your respective organizations including challenges and successes as well as your assessment of the U.S. Government's level of prioritization and funding of democracy and governance programming.

I also would be interested in hearing your assessment of which of the upcoming African elections pose the greatest challenges in terms of funding, logistics, internal political dynamics or conflict-related concerns. With over 30 Presidential and parliamentary elections taking place in Africa between now and the end of 2016, today's hearing couldn't have been more timely as nations such as Nigeria, Sudan, and the DRC prepare to go to the polls in 2015. I am not only concerned with transparency, accountability, and human security in those specific national elections, but also their impacts on regional stability.

As noted earlier, while elections are important, we know they are singular events in the electoral cycle, so it is my hope that U.S. support for these efforts is inclusive of pre-election assistance related to access, safety, and integrity of ballots. One of the on-going concerns I always have is that in some of the countries where we are not clear where the next level of leadership is going to come from, what is the U.S. doing to help to contribute to that leadership development?

Lastly, as we look across the political landscape of the continent, there seems to be an upward trend in the number of incumbent leaders attempting constitutional amendments to extend their terms in office. It would be helpful if all of us could elaborate on this issue and its implications for the future of governance on the continent.

And in closing, it is vital that the U.S. maintains its commitment to peaceful, credible, and transparent elections in Africa. And it is now up to each of us to ensure effective coordination, improved diplomatic relations, and the transfer of the expertise and resources to realize these ends. Thank you and I yield back.

Mr. EMMER. The Chair recognizes Representative Meadows for his opening remarks.

Mr. MEADOWS. Thank you, Mr. Chairman and I thank the ranking member, Ms. Bass, for her leadership on this particular issue. I am going to apologize up front. I have got another hearing and then some budget issues that I am having to deal with this morning. But I do plan to stay and the reason I am here, honestly, is to try to not only augment what Chairman Smith and Ranking Member Bass continue to do in terms of our outreach with regards to the African continent, but specifically those—I enjoy a great relationship with many of our African Ambassadors. And our involvement there is critical. I think it is one of the areas that has the most potential, but probably has the most work to do as well. And so it is my hope that we can hear from you and your testimony and then hopefully with some follow-up questions together that we will do this in a bipartisan way to figure out the best way to move forward in the continent.

Thank you so much. I will yield back, Mr. Chairman.

Mr. EMMER. Thank you. Mr. Eric Postel became USAID's Assistant Administrator for the Bureau of Economic Growth, Education, and Environment in March 2011. In October 2014, he was asked by the USAID Administrator to serve as the Assistant to the Administrator for Africa. Mr. Postel brings to the position more than 25 years of private-sector experience working in emerging markets, especially those in Africa. He also has founded an investment banking and consulting firm, focusing on emerging markets, worked for Citibank Tokyo, and served as a commissioner on the U.S. Helping to Enhance the Livelihood of People Around the Globe Commission.

Mr. Postel, welcome to the committee.

STATEMENT OF THE HONORABLE ERIC G. POSTEL, ASSISTANT TO THE ADMINISTRATOR, BUREAU FOR AFRICA, U.S. AGENCY FOR INTERNATIONAL DEVELOPMENT

Mr. POSTEL. Thank you, Mr. Chairman, Ranking Member Bass, and members of the subcommittee. Thank you very much for your welcome and for the opportunity to appear before you today. And I ask that my full testimony be entered into the record.

The U.S. Agency for International Development promotes better governance as an integral part of our Agency's mission. Supporting elections and political processes have been a cornerstone of our work in Africa for more than two decades. During the last 6 years alone, USAID has worked to improve the credibility and conduct of elections in at least 34 countries in Africa.

As you know, USAID's electoral assistance can take multiple forms. I will mention six of them: One, building the institutional capacity of electoral commissions; two, helping to strengthen political parties; three, training media on how to report responsibly; four, encouraging and promoting peaceful, nonviolent participation by the citizenry of the country; five, facilitating the inclusion of women, youth, and people with disabilities at all stages of the process; and/or six, equipping nonpartisan election monitors and observers.

We do much of this work by supporting international organizations including those who are testifying here today and they have a very long and expert experience in these areas. We also are increasingly partnering directly with local, nonpartisan, civil society organizations and networks on election observation and voter outreach such as NGO 3D in Senegal and government institutions such as electoral commissions in Ghana and elsewhere.

In Zambia's recent election earlier this year, USAID provided critical support to the civil society, to the election commission, and thousands of nonpartisan citizen observers who monitored the conduct of the elections and conducted a sophisticated parallel vote tabulation that confirmed the official close, and I mean under 10,000 vote, difference in the results.

In Burundi, where political violence remains a serious concern, our support typifies what we see as the best practice of starting to work long before the campaigning even begins. Soon after the completion of the last elections in 2010, we began a series of assessments to understand what the situation had evolved to, the needs, and to identify possible useful interventions so that by April 2013, we had launched programs pointing toward this year's election.

And in Nigeria, in close partnership with the United Kingdom's Department of International Development, we are supporting a whole host of Nigerian efforts on elections. Our work in elections administration supports the operations of what is called the INEC, Independent National Election Commission. To date, they have distributed 55 million voter cards to more than 80 percent of the registered voters, a huge improvement over 2011. The INEC's election support centers will monitor the deployment of materials and collection of ballots.

We and our partners have also been working with youth to support their participation in the processes and working as hard as we possibly can to promote peaceful elections. Lastly, we are strengthening Nigerian civil society's efforts to hold candidates, parties, the INEC, and other officials accountable by observing and reporting out on their own elections. Our partners are training and deploying more than 3,000 domestic observers for the Presidential election. However, U.S. Government support alone cannot determine the success of an election, particularly when leaders ignore or rewrite the rules, or deliberately weaken their own institutions to serve their own interests.

Organizing and conducting credible, legitimate, and peaceful elections is not without challenges as you referenced. One of the key lessons we have learned is that strong institutions and the actual elections are mutually reinforcing. Elections are only one step in the long process, as you alluded to, that is required for true democratic transformation. We aim for our electoral programs to contribute to the whole process, not just election day. And it is sustained support for the process of democracy from the halls of the government and the capital to the village council and across all the full range of citizens' groups and independent voices is critical to creating and sustaining an environment where democracy can grow and thrive.

USAID and its partners have been fortunate to receive strong support and guidance from this subcommittee and its hardworking staff which allows us to pursue this important work.

Thank you for the opportunity to testify this morning. I look forward to your questions and also to hearing the thoughts of the experts on the next panel. Thank you.

[The prepared statement of Mr. Postel follows:]

Testimony by United States Agency for International Development
Assistant to the Administrator for Africa Eric Postel
House Subcommittee for Africa, Global Health,
Global Human Rights and International Organizations
March 18, 2015

"U.S. Election Support in Africa"

Chairman Smith, Ranking Member Bass, and Members of the Subcommittee, thank you for the opportunity to appear before you today.

When I last spoke with this Subcommittee in November, we discussed one of the most pressing challenges facing the continent, reducing energy poverty. Today, we've come together to address another critical undertaking that holds the potential to impact the continent's future for generations to come - credible and legitimate elections. Our Agency mission statement, "We partner to end extreme poverty, and promote resilient, democratic societies while advancing our security and prosperity," reflects the importance we place on this topic.

While visiting Ghana in 2009, President Obama observed that, "Development depends on good governance. That is the ingredient which has been missing in far too many places, for far too long. That's the change that can unlock Africa's potential." Consistent with the President's vision, the United States Agency for International Development (USAID) promotes better governance as an integral part of our development agenda. But the real story isn't one of our technical assistance or support for elections. The real story lies in the committed African men and women that are working every day to strengthen their nations' democratic institutions and processes. According to a 2014 Afrobarometer survey, seven out of ten Africans prefer democracy to other political systems. These individuals, growing in number, making their voices heard -- through elections and through civil society organizations -- are the faces of democracy in Africa.

Dedicated civil servants like Justice Irene Mambilima, a member of Zambia's Electoral Commission who I had the privilege to meet and see in action, are the backbone of democracy. She, alongside countless other Zambians, worked determinedly following the death of President Michael Sata last October to prepare the country for a presidential by-election within the three-month period mandated by the constitution. It was clear to me that she and her fellow commissioners were as fiercely determined as Zambia's citizens to make democracy work, and were striving tirelessly to put together a free, credible, and peaceful, nationwide election in record time. Africans such as these Zambians, some prominent, others working behind the scenes, are writing the story of Africa's future. Supporting their efforts is USAID's goal.

Since the early 1990s, USAID has promoted political freedom as an indispensable part of development. We are guided in these efforts by our Democracy, Human Rights and Governance Strategy which highlights participation, inclusion, transparency, and accountability as principles central to the achievement of human rights, democratic governance, and sustainable development. These principles are vital to the pursuit of freedom, national security and economic development.

Today, I will highlight USAID's support for elections and political processes which in turn helps establish and consolidate inclusive, accountable, and resilient democratic societies that advance freedom, dignity and development on the continent. I will provide examples of our support, highlight lessons learned, and address the challenges moving forward.

USAID Support

Supporting elections and political processes has been a cornerstone of USAID's work in Africa for more than two decades. During the Obama Administration alone, USAID and its international and local partners have worked to improve the credibility and conduct of elections in at least 34 countries in sub-Saharan Africa. In Kenya, USAID was actively engaged with myriad Kenyan stakeholders, other donors, and across the interagency from the 2007 -2008 post-election violence period through the adoption of the 2010 Constitution, through the 2013 6-ballot general election; our robust support assisted Kenyans to conduct civic education on decentralization and the new multiple-ballot vote, to identify and mitigate conflict triggers, and to peacefully resolve electoral disputes. In Kenya, Liberia, Nigeria, and a handful of other countries, we have worked across multiple electoral cycles during that period. This fact alone underscores one of the key democratic achievements in Africa: elections have become a regular, predictable feature of politics across the region. In a growing number of countries such as Botswana, Cape Verde, and Mauritius, free, fair and credible elections have taken place for years without substantial assistance from donors. In fact, our programs increasingly support training by experts from these countries, and others like Ghana, Senegal, and South Africa, who are sharing their countries' own substantial expertise and lessons learned with their peers in developing democracies around the world. As we reflect on the challenges facing individual countries at any given moment, it's important not to lose sight of these longer-term positive trends across Africa when it comes to elections and political processes.

Yet elections alone do not make a democracy or even assure democratic transformation; they are a snapshot of democratic trends, not the whole story. That is why we also work to ensure that the enabling conditions for successful elections are in place, to strengthen the rule of law, to promote and protect human rights, to improve governance institutions and processes, support a dynamic civil society, and promote a free and independent media. These elements of democratic governance are just as important as the ballot box and help reinforce the important electoral cycle that plays out between polls and sustain democratic reforms. Voices need to be heard, systems need to function, impartial justice needs to be dispensed, and human rights need to be protected *every day*, not just on Election Day. This is the foundation for long-term democratic change.

Our support of credible and legitimate elections provides a crucial opportunity for citizens to hold their political leaders accountable and to give ordinary citizens a role in determining the future of their nations through peaceful political competition. Through diplomacy and development assistance, the United States remains committed to supporting credible, transparent, and inclusive elections, encouraging a respect for the political rules of the game, and reducing the likelihood of electoral violence. Our activities in support of credible elections typically include: providing assistance to election management bodies; strengthening the capacity of political parties to develop and campaign on issue-based platforms and to accurately represent their constituents' interests; and supporting civil society's efforts to bolster civic and voter education, and to conduct oversight of the democratic process.

Very importantly, our goal is to support the creation of fair and credible electoral systems, not to determine the winners of elections. We strive only for legitimate, impartial, and peaceful political processes, not particular outcomes. We support the right of leaders to govern, but only if they win elections fair and square. Incumbents in several African countries, however, have no interest in receiving international assistance that aims to improve the quality and credibility of elections. Fear of losing power motivates them to manipulate laws, institutions, and processes to create a playing field so uneven that their opponents stand no chance of winning, even when a majority of citizens would support them. In these cases, USAID works closely with the State Department, other donors, local media, and civil society to try to create an environment for reforms that will lead to more credible electoral processes.

A vibrant and empowered civil society helps to promote inclusiveness, transparency, rule of law and human rights, and acts as a partner to governments and the private sector in delivering services. As African societies and political systems continue to develop, the expectations of people toward their governments continue to rise. Whereas an Afrobarometer survey in 2000 of citizens in 34 African countries showed that they believed the degree of democracy was based on the performance of the president, the 2011-2013 survey showed that they now believe the leading factor is the quality of elections. A robust and energized civil society is also a key ingredient as governments consider reforms to electoral legal frameworks, for monitoring the entire electoral cycle, and for observing processes and outcomes on Election Day itself.

Countries with strong democratic institutions and processes that uphold the rule of law and respect citizens have greater success in mitigating conflict, ensuring security and promoting sustainable development and prosperity.[i] In addition to supporting electoral processes and civil society, USAID electoral assistance builds the institutional capacity of electoral commissions;

strengthens political parties; equips non-partisan election monitors and observers; trains media on how to report responsibly; promotes peaceful, non-violent participation; and facilitates the inclusion of women, youth, and people with disabilities at all stages of the electoral process.

We do much of this work by supporting international partners like the International Republican Institute, the National Democratic Institute, and the International Foundation for Electoral Systems, which have a long history of expertise in this arena, some of whose leaders are here with us today. We also increasingly partner directly with local non-partisan civil society organizations and networks on election observation and voter outreach, such as NGO3D in Senegal, and government institutions such as Ghana's Electoral Commission. As highlighted during the President's 2013 visit to Africa, USAID also supports innovative partnerships such as the one between the University of Southern Africa and the South African Independent Election Commission to improve the capacity of election officials across the region with hands-on and distance learning courses.

Although we read and hear narratives to the contrary, we've contributed to and seen a number of recent electoral successes, and believe with targeted support, more are on the horizon.

In Zambia recently, even pouring rains and rising flood waters did not prevent many Zambians from venturing out to their polling places to exercise their right to select their new leader. The results speak for themselves. Despite the stormy weather and an extremely close race — only 27,000 votes separated the two candidates — the Commission was able to tally the results and officially declare an uncontested winner in just four days, with few disruptions or incidents of violence.

Indeed, the electoral authorities were only one part of the successful process. USAID provided critical support to civil society and thousands of nonpartisan citizen-observers who monitored the conduct of the elections and conducted a sophisticated parallel vote tabulation that confirmed the official results. In defense of their interests, political party poll watchers observed at voting sites and helped validate result tabulations.

These rigorous, transparent procedures provided confidence in the democratic process. These elections benefited from experience: Zambia has a history of hotly contested elections and peaceful transitions of power ever since President Kaunda yielded to popular demands and stepped down in 1991. While some observers noted that there could be improvements in the future, most agreed that the elections were free, peaceful and credible. Zambia made the process look relatively easy, but elections are, in fact, a complex undertaking. The process begins long before Election Day and endures well beyond the moment the last ballot is counted.

In addition to continued engagement with Zambia, USAID is working with electoral officials, political parties, and civic activists to prepare for upcoming polls in several other countries, including Nigeria, Burundi, Cote d'Ivoire, Burkina Faso and the Democratic Republic of Congo. In each case, citizens are eager to exercise their right to vote.

In Burundi, where political violence remains a serious concern, USAID's support for peaceful and credible elections typifies the best practice of starting such work long before the campaigning begins. Soon after the conclusion of the 2010 elections, which brought the post-conflict transition government established by the Arusha Accords to an end, we commenced a series of assessments to understand the electoral landscape, identify needs, and recommend possible interventions. By April 2013, we launched programs to encourage inclusive dialogue around the 2015 elections as a proactive way of addressing concerns about political violence. Since then, USAID has supported efforts to foster an inclusive political climate ahead of Burundi's presidential, parliamentary, and local elections cycle, which will begin later this spring. By working with local partners, our programs encourage a culture of inclusive dialogue and democracy, based on the principles of mutual respect and tolerance enshrined in Burundi's Constitution and the Arusha Peace and Reconciliation Agreement. Our programs support civic education, media, peaceful youth engagement in elections, conflict early warning and response systems, and technical assistance to the Independent National Electoral Commission.

Former U.S. Special Envoy for the Great Lakes Region and the Democratic Republic of the Congo, Russ Feingold said in February that the "United States is urging the Burundian government to ensure that the upcoming elections are consistent with the Arusha Accords, which state unambiguously that no president shall serve more than two terms. It is our belief that upholding Arusha, including its provision on term limits, is key to maintaining a still fragile stability in Burundi in the near-term." USAID and its partners in Burundi are poised to adapt and respond to the changing political environment. At the moment, we are focused on training of local observers, conflict monitoring, media training, peacebuilding activities, voter education, and providing economic opportunities that reduce youth vulnerability to political manipulation. The international community and civil society continue to monitor the voter registration process. Fortunately, despite some shortcomings, so far, the voter registration process has proceeded peacefully. Nevertheless, we are also supporting local organizations that monitor and report on any human rights abuses that could occur around the elections.

By far the most consequential election this year in Africa will take place in Nigeria. Peaceful and credible elections are crucial to development in Africa's most populous country, and these upcoming elections are likely to be among the most competitive in the country's 55-year history. In fact, Afrobarometer's December 2014 public opinion survey showed the two presidential candidates – President Goodluck Jonathan and opposition candidate Muhammadu Buhari – in a dead heat. Since then, the Boko Haram insurgency has complicated the election by decreasing security in the North East and creating more than 1.2 million internally displaced persons[ii].

The United States continues to strongly believe that free, fair and transparent elections in Nigeria are essential. Secretary of State Kerry stated last month that the United States was deeply disappointed by the decision to postpone the elections from February 14 to March 28. I want to use this opportunity to reinforce the importance of ensuring that there are no further delays. I will be traveling late next week with Assistant Secretary of State Linda Thomas-Greenfield to Nigeria prior to the elections. The international community will be watching closely to see if the Nigerian government maintains its commitment to guarantee voter security and access to the polls to the maximum extent possible, including in the North East Zone, and accurately counts the votes cast throughout the country.

USAID's current assistance to Nigeria draws upon best practices and lessons learned from more than 15 consecutive years of elections support to that country. In close partnership with the United Kingdom's Department for International Development and other donors, we support Nigerian efforts to professionalize electoral administration, address electoral conflict and reduce violence, increase participation of marginalized voters, and professionalize political parties. We also support civil society's efforts to observe the electoral environment and the actual polling, independently verify vote counts, and promote peaceful participation.

Our work in electoral administration supports the operations of the Independent National Election Commission, or INEC. INEC's objective is to improve the quality of the elections while cultivating public confidence in credible processes and their outcomes. Our assistance strengthens INEC's capacity to train an estimated 1.2 million permanent and ad-hoc electoral staff; coordinate security planning; improve communications, voter education, and public outreach; and create more effective election dispute resolution mechanisms. Across Nigeria's 36 states, INEC's Election Operations Support Centers will monitor the deployment of materials and collection of ballots. To date, INEC has distributed 55 million voter cards to just over 80 percent of registered voters – a huge improvement over the 2011 elections, which many observers called the most credible in Nigeria's history.

While support for institutions is important, we are also focused on promoting non-violence, acknowledging that the 2011 elections were the most violent in Nigeria's history, with 800 fatalities in the immediate post-election period and over 65,000 displaced.[iii] USAID and its partners have been supporting youth participation in political processes and the promotion of peaceful elections. In late 2014, we helped launch a "Vote - Not Fight" campaign with the headlining support of non-partisan Nigerian musicians such as rapper *2face Idibia* and other celebrities, as well as political leaders who signed a non-violence pledge called the Abuja

Accord. These activities both get out the youth vote and advocate for non-violent participation in Nigeria's democracy.

Lastly, we are strengthening Nigerian civil society's efforts to hold candidates, parties, the INEC, and other officials accountable by observing and reporting out on their own elections. Our partners are training and deploying more than 3,000 domestic observers for the rescheduled March 2015 presidential election. These observers are trained in how to conduct a "quick count," which is a systematic observation methodology that independently measures the quality of election-day processes and official voting results. We've also helped create a conflict early warning system that has deployed 774 locally recruited observers in every single local government area in Nigeria since last November. They will provide information on emerging trends that are likely to impact electoral processes and risks for conflict through bi-weekly critical incidents reports in the pre-election period.

Challenges and Lessons Learned

Organizing and conducting credible, legitimate, and peaceful elections is not without its challenges. While ordinary Africans appeal for transparent elections and leadership accountability, too many political leaders continue to manipulate the electoral process, challenge constitutionally mandated term limits, and use other undemocratic means to maintain a grip on power. According to Freedom House, the average tenure for leaders in "not free" countries is 18 years, whereas in "free" or "partly free" countries, the average is less than five years. While the number of long-ruling African "Big Men" is declining, ten leaders today have been in power over 20 years.[iv] President Obama noted while in Ghana that history is not on the side of those who use coups or change constitutions to remain in power, he posed that, "Africa needs strong institutions, not strongmen."

In response to this challenge, one of the key lessons we've learned is that strong institutions and credible elections tend to be mutually reinforcing. In several countries in sub-Saharan Africa, political parties and leaders who have pursued politics as a zero-sum game are gradually being replaced by a new generation of leaders with greater trust in the rule of law and in the non-partisan, independent institutions that conduct and oversee elections. In Mozambique and Namibia, voters recently elected new presidents after the incumbents retired in accordance with their constitutionally-mandated term limits. One of these statesmen, former Namibian President Pohamba, recently won the Mo Ibrahim prize for good governance.

In contrast, where leaders try to cling to power, their actions can backfire and create costly and unnecessary political crises that threaten years of development progress. Last October, 200,000 people in Burkina Faso took to the streets to protest now former President Blaise Compaoré's plan to circumvent his term limits. USAID is providing support to Burkina's transitional government, civil society organizations, the independent electoral commission, and political parties to hold presidential elections and restore democratic governance. Yet this example points to another critical lesson for the U.S. Government and its partners: our support alone cannot determine the success of an election, particularly when leaders ignore or rewrite the rules, and deliberately weaken their own institutions, to serve their own interests.

This delicate balance between powerful leaders and their interests on the one hand, and the need for strong and independent institutions on the other, highlights the key to USAID's approach to elections. We aim for our elections programs to contribute to the entire political process, not just the immediate event on Election Day. Our work in Zambia, Burundi and Nigeria demonstrates that long-term engagement over several years can be enormously helpful in developing those institutions needed to keep political systems resilient in the face of unexpected shocks like the death of a president or an armed insurgency, or long-simmering issues, like ethnic violence and corruption. USAID and its partners have been fortunate to receive strong support and guidance from this Subcommittee that allows us to pursue this important work.

Conclusion
A few decades ago, many African politicians and their supporters blamed the United States and other Western democracies for imposing unrealistic standards on their governments and political systems. But today, African citizens point to the examples of countries like Zambia, Ghana, Benin, and Namibia, to claim democracy as an effective model for Africa. Elections are only one step in a long process that is required for true democratic transformation. Indeed, sustained support for the process of democracy—from the halls of government in the capital to the village council, and across the full range of citizens groups and other independent voices in between— will be critical to creating and sustaining an environment where it can grow and thrive.

Thank you for the opportunity to testify this afternoon. I look forward to your questions.

---

[i] Radelet, Steven, *Emerging Africa: How 17 Countries are Leading the Way*, Center for Global Development, 2010
[ii] International Organization for Migration http://www.iom.int/cms/en/sites/iom/home/news-and-views/press-briefing-notes/pbn-2015/pbn-listing/boko-haram-may-have-displaced-ov.html
[iii] Human Rights Watch http://www.hrw.org/news/2011/05/16/nigeria-post-election-violence-killed-800
[iv] Freedom House presentation at USAID in February 2015 cited 10 leaders in power more than 20 years, and an additional four leaders more than 14 years (Republic of Congo - Brazzaville, Djibouti, Rwanda, DRC).

Mr. EMMER. Thank you, Mr. Postel.

Before we proceed to questions, Mr. Bera has joined the committee and I wanted to offer him the opportunity to make any opening remarks he might have.

Mr. BERA. I am perfectly happy to proceed to questions.

Mr. EMMER. Okay, great. All right, then I will recognize myself for questions.

Mr. Postel, you went through the six things that USAID does to encourage a safe and viable, valid electoral process, and then you came back to it with respect to Nigeria in your comments right toward the end when you referenced ''we are committed and working toward promoting peaceful, nonviolent, electoral processes.'' And then that was number four, and I have summarized it a little bit differently, but that was the gist. And then number five was ''encouraging the participation of young people and women in the process.'' I want to focus on those two in the brief time that we have this morning. Maybe Nigeria is a good place to focus since we have got the election that has been rescheduled from February 14th to March 28th.

First off, the postponement, I am going to throw in one little curve, too, because you said at the end, ''the process depends upon''—I am going to paraphrase it. USAID can only do so much. It really depends on leaders who do not ignore or rewrite the rules. Can you give us a little bit more insight as to the specific situation in Nigeria with the postponement and then I want to come back and ask you to address numbers four and five a little bit more, both with respect to Nigeria and more broadly.

Mr. POSTEL. Thank you for the question, Congressman. As you probably saw, the State Department issued a statement that they were disappointed by the delay, but the announcement was that they basically weren't ready and they needed more time. And that was the Government of Nigeria's decision. At this stage, with that as a fait accompli, our focus is to continue to say that the U.S. Government feels very strongly that we don't want any more delays and we really do hope that this delay has been put to good use, to make sure that they are ready and in terms of the mechanics of the election and also to try to do everything possible to deal with some of the side effects of the problems related to Boko Haram and so forth.

So for instance, there are, I believe, close to 1 million internally-displaced people, people that are not in their homes. And we have certainly been trying to support the electoral commission with ideas about how to enable those people to vote and maximize the ability of all Nigerians across the whole country to vote. And so we are working hard to support them in their efforts to have this happen in barely 2 weeks.

Mr. EMMER. Thank you. Back to leaders who ignore or rewrite the rules. So that wasn't the situation that we were talking about in terms of leadership in Nigeria postponing this. This is USAID. From your perspective, this was their taking control of their own situation, saying they weren't ready, and postponing it for, until further notice, legitimate reasons.

Mr. POSTEL. That is what they told us and they set a date and if they stick to that, I think that we can move forward, that they felt they needed that time to finish their preparation.

Mr. EMMER. And as far as USAID, your involvement, because we heard this back in early February, that you were training 3,000 some folks to be involved in the process. That was ready to go on the 14th when it was originally scheduled?

Mr. POSTEL. I believe it was, Congressman.

Mr. EMMER. Now to the two specific things. How do you, USAID, how does USAID encourage and specific examples if you will, and if Nigeria is a place to focus on, that is fine, but pick whatever you want. How do you encourage a peaceful process?

Mr. POSTEL. Thank you for your question. It is more art than science, but it is something that is very important to do. And there are a number of examples. It is not one specific thing. One of the things is to encourage a lot of people to have dialogue and to get a lot of people in the country trying to talk about the advantages and why peaceful resolution of issues is a much better way to go. And this——

Mr. EMMER. Can I?

Mr. POSTEL. Sure.

Mr. EMMER. How do you do that?

Mr. POSTEL. So we try to work with a lot of different parts of society. We have on occasion worked with people that are in the arts who the youth might look up to. We have worked extensively in some countries with faith-based groups. In fact, in Nigeria, there is a coalition of Christians and Muslims who are working in an interfaith center and they are speaking out about this and trying to encourage it.

I understand that all the media have agreed that some time next week there is going to be a day where basically this message of nonviolent elections is going to be on all channels, talked about all day long, so anybody who has got access to any media in the country. So what happens is that people just work through many different channels of civil society.

Of course, the U.S. Government speaks directly about these subjects, but I think one of the lessons learned over time, is it is better when the citizens of their own country speak to their fellow citizens, rather than us across the oceans and so forth.

Mr. EMMER. I understand that Gretchen Birkle of IRI will testify that roughly a dozen African nations that are holding elections this year, they are engaged in civil conflicts or battling terrorism or domestic insurgencies. You have given me some of it, I think just now, but what is the USAID policy for supporting elections in countries like this beyond what you have just talked about?

Mr. POSTEL. Thank you for question, Congressman. That is a great question because it is a very challenging situation and what we have to do is on the one hand it presents an opportunity to talk to people in these countries where there is instability or conflict, that peaceful, nonviolent means of resolving disputes and having those discussions through civil society discussions and through elections is a much better way to go. And so because there are disagreements, it is a chance to really work on that message and help people learn how to have those dialogues and encourage the democratic processes.

But, of course, we also have to factor in safety to our own staff and our partners. And in some cases, we are able to reconcile both. There have been some cases where we are not able to perhaps work in an entire country because of the need to worry about the safety of our partners or our own staff. So that is the biggest challenge to it which is the safety side. But there are also opportunities to show people there is actually a better way and try to work with a lot of voices and to not let the rabble-rousers and violent extremists control the narrative and drive people more and more toward violence.

Mr. EMMER. Thank you and I thank the ranking member for her patience. One last one before I turn it over to her. The recommendations for governments of national unity have been widely utilized to redress election misfires. However, can you suggest any situation in which such blended governments have succeeded when the main opposition opponent has been included in a blended government?

Mr. POSTEL. I am not expert enough to be able to answer that, but I will be happy to come back to you. It is not an area that I am familiar with. Thank you for the question.

[The information referred to follows:]

WRITTEN RESPONSE RECEIVED FROM THE HONORABLE ERIC G. POSTEL TO QUESTION ASKED DURING THE HEARING BY THE HONORABLE TOM EMMER

Governments of National Unity (GNUs), by this and other names, have been employed in Africa during post-conflict transitions, as in South Africa, Sudan, Burundi, and the Democratic Republic of Congo. More recently, countries such as Kenya and Zimbabwe have used GNUs as a temporary mechanism to restore governance after electoral disputes. This approach has proven useful in the short term for conflict mitigation, particularly when the GNU period is relatively brief. Yet over time, these arrangements tend to undermine good governance principles and practices, while postponing or even exacerbating the political grievances they were meant to resolve.

American University scholar Carl LeVan has studied the topic and summarized his findings as follows:

> Power sharing agreements have been widely used in Africa as paths out of civil war. However the research focus on conflict mitigation provides an inadequate guide to recent cases such as Kenya and Zimbabwe. When used in response to flawed elections, pacts guaranteeing political inclusion adversely affect government performance and democratization. Political inclusion in these cases undermines vertical relationships of accountability, increases budgetary spending, and creates conditions for policy gridlock.

Dr. LeVan's paper and analysis is available at: http://onlinelibrary.wiley.com/doi/10.1111/j.1468-0491.2010.01514.x/abstract

Mr. EMMER. Thank you. And if you do have something after, please supply it. At this point, I will recognize the ranking member for her questions.

Ms. BASS. Thank you, Mr. Chair. I just have a couple of quick questions. One, you were making reference to media in Nigeria and you were talking about questions calling for it to be peaceful. Is that an effort that either is one that we are paying for or subcontracting with or were you just making reference to an effort that is happening in Nigeria?

Mr. POSTEL. Thank you for your question, Congresswoman. We are not paying for the media, but our partners have been involved in encouraging that this might occur. But Nigerians are making this happen to the best of my knowledge.

Ms. BASS. Okay, I wanted to know if you could elaborate where USAID is currently prioritizing democracy and governance programs amongst its varied objectives. Specifically, what kind of election assistance does the U.S. support in Africa and where is USAID focusing? I am a proud member of NED's Board, so I am aware of that piece. But outside of NED, what does USAID—in which countries?

Mr. POSTEL. Thank you for the question, Congressman. I can get you a complete list, but off the top of my head I believe this year we are working on a total of 13 or 15 different elections, most of which are national level. Some of the big countries—some of the countries where we have the biggest activities right now include the Democratic Republic of the Congo, Nigeria, Kenya, and so forth. We can get you a full list. But it is not all inclusive because, for instance, we just supported the snap election that occurred in Zambia as a result of the death of the head of state.

Ms. BASS. Right.

Mr. POSTEL. So the list, of course, varies year to year, as we try to maximize the efficiency of the resources and adjust that to deal with the electoral calendar.

[The information referred to follows:]

WRITTEN RESPONSE RECEIVED FROM THE HONORABLE ERIC G. POSTEL TO QUESTION ASKED DURING THE HEARING BY THE HONORABLE KAREN BASS

The below table notes in which African countries/operating units USAID had programs addressing democracy and governance issues in 2014. It also notes where elections-related programs in particular were active.

Operating Units working on Elections, Political Processes, or Consensus-Building Programs specifically (XE) or Democracy & Governance and/or related Conflict Mitigation Programs generally (X) in 2014	
Angola	X
Burundi	XE
Cameroon	
Central African Republic	X
Chad	
Cote d'Ivoire	XE
Democratic Republic of the Congo	XE
Djibouti	
Ethiopia	X
Gabon	
Ghana	XE
Guinea	X
Kenya	X
Lesotho	XE
Liberia	XE
Malawi	X
Mali	XE
Mauritania	
Mozambique	X
Niger	X
Nigeria	XE
Rwanda	X
Senegal	XE
Sierra Leone	
Somalia	XE
South Sudan	XE
Sudan	XE
Swaziland	X
Tanzania	XE
Togo	
Uganda	XE
Zambia	XE
Zimbabwe	XE
African Union	
USAID Africa Regional	X
USAID East Africa Regional	X
USAID Southern Africa Regional	XE
USAID West Africa Regional	XE

Ms. BASS. And speaking about the resources, can you speak to trends for funding for democracy and governance programming within USAID? I have heard, and I don't know what the exact figures are, that it has diminished in previous years.

Mr. POSTEL. Thank you for your question, Congressman. There was some decline. We are still spending quite a bit of funds on these topics. In the President's FY 16 budget, he requested a total of $300 million for Africa on democracy and governance of which $62 million would go for the general topic of elections and consensus building.

Ms. BASS. You know, do we spend any time, and I am just thinking that the country of Namibia and you mentioned Zambia, you know, there are examples in Africa where there have been a sound process, you know, where the transfer of governance has been peaceful, has been consistent. And we tend to always talk about the problems. So my question to you is, does USAID spend any time promoting the good examples? I know there is going to be an inauguration in Namibia in just a couple of days, but we do tend to just focus on that and I don't know if we spend any time talking about positives.

Mr. POSTEL. Congressman, you see me smiling ear to ear because in November I was in Zambia to work on things relating to economic growth and I also met with the electoral commission and looked at what support we were gave. And then I watched what happened. And I felt so strongly on this point that you made that I suggested to our teams that I would author an article which we put into several African press outlets to basically talk about the success in Zambia. I am not saying that it was flawless, but the trend was right. There are other examples such as Namibia that you mentioned.

Even Kenya, if you think about it, what went on in the most recent election which incidentally, Congressman, there was huge work on a massive scale. I mean 1 million-plus youth. It was a huge amount of work done in Kenya, right from the end of the disastrous 2007 election to try to prepare through the whole cycle. And so it was a lot better election. So I fully agree with you that we need to talk about these because I think they represent strong models for the other countries and let them realize that number one, it can be done because as you know, pulling off elections is actually logistically complicated and for some of these countries they are very young countries, so let them know what is possible and that the world commends those who can pull it off. So I personally think that we have to do more and I am dedicated to doing more, to trumpet the success so that we shine a light on that so others can see what is possible.

Ms. BASS. And you know, I think that is very good and I would appreciate in the future you letting us know what you have done in that regard and then how we might be supportive. But just like I think it is important that we publicize that within Africa, I also think it is important for us because you know, when we talk about Africa it is always from the point of view of some problems, so I think here amongst our colleagues it is important. But I think that is our responsibility. We can spread the word on that.

So with that, Mr. Chair, I will yield.

Mr. EMMER. Thank you. The Chair now recognizes, Mr. Meadows.

Mr. MEADOWS. Thank you, Mr. Chairman. Thank you for your testimony so far and I agree with the ranking member that we need to do a better job of telling the positive things. Some of us represent districts where supporting Africa and foreign aid and those kind of things gets us reelected. I am not one that enjoys that particular constituency. I would assure you. At the same time, I have been willing to invest political capital on this particular issue and it is mainly out of my respect for the ranking member and the chairman and their work in this area and my love for many of the people, many of whom I have met for the first time, but having traveled to Africa a number of times and worked alongside of orphanages or schools or other people in need, it is critical.

So I say that with the backdrop because I want to focus on a couple of areas that knowing that you have a willing participant here, there are some areas that I am extremely concerned about that I would like for either you to address or for you to take back to the appropriate people to address. One is obviously a USAID diplomat was arrested at the DRC within the last couple of days, on Sunday. You know, this is one that really, I think, comes under your supervision from a USG point of view. And here we have a U.S. diplomat being arrested in a country in which we are involved with, so can you help us understand the events and has there been follow-up calls with them and what should we expect?

Mr. POSTEL. Thank you for your question, Congressman, and also for your support in an environment where not everybody agrees with some of this work.

So the individual who is a Foreign Service Officer was at an event that was meant, per our prior discussion, to encourage youth to peacefully air their differences and peacefully participate in electoral processes. There were a number of people taken into custody at that event by the secret services of the government there and it took 3 hours until our diplomat could be released. And I was working on it as it was happening as was everybody there.

Our Ambassador to the Democratic Republic of the Congo was fully engaged as was the head of USAID's office there and the whole team. In a follow up, once that person was released, they have already met with the Minister of Foreign Affairs and had a discussion and expressed our unhappiness with what happened.

Mr. MEADOWS. I hope expressed our strong disapproval.

Mr. POSTEL. Yes, sir. Exactly. And the conversations are not finished. There was also some inaccurate reporting in the press about what this event was and people are working with the press and talking to people to clarify their understandings because it was not as some portrayed it, some attempt by the opposition party to somehow cause trouble. That is not at all what it was.

Mr. MEADOWS. Alright, so let me follow up a little bit then because I think the message needs to be clear. There is a finite amount of resources and you have to make a decision each and every time where you are going to deploy those resources. A willing or at least an open government that respects the diplomatic security that comes along with that is a key component for any of us and we have to make decisions. And so we want to hear back from you on the results of those follow-up conversations if you will report back to the chairman and this committee on that particular aspect of that so that we make sure that no one is in harm's way. God forbid that it could have been much worse than what we saw.

[The information referred to follows:]

WRITTEN RESPONSE RECEIVED FROM THE HONORABLE ERIC G. POSTEL TO QUESTION ASKED DURING THE HEARING BY THE HONORABLE MARK MEADOWS

Mr. Kevin Sturr, Director of the USAID/DRC Democracy, Human Rights and Governance office was detained on March 15 after attending a press conference organized by a group of civic activists to discuss their new youth movement called "Filimbi" ("whistle blower" in Swahili). The press conference followed a workshop with civil society members and musician activists, including two Young African Leadership Initiative (YALI) fellows and other YALI network members. Members of Senegalese youth movement Y'en a Marre and Burkina Faso youth movement Balai Citoyen were also present and detained along with the owners of the venue. The event was sponsored in part by the Embassy's Public Affairs Section. USAID did not financially support the event.

Mr. Sturr was released unharmed several hours after his arrest following an inquiry by the U.S. Embassy in Kinshasa. The U.S. Embassy protested the detention of U.S. diplomat Kevin Sturr to the Ministry of Foreign Affairs in the DRC and to the DRC Ambassador in the United States. In a discussion with the U.S. Ambassador, the Congolese intelligence agency indicated that they would complete and submit the findings of their investigation of Mr. Sturr by Friday, March 20 to the President. As of this writing (March 27), the government's determination in this matter is unknown and Mr. Sturr's passport remains with the Congolese authorities.

Congolese press reports that some members of the Congolese National Assembly have called for the release of Congolese youth who were detained. The President of the National Assembly is acting to keep Members of Parliament (MPs) informed on the matter. Congolese press further reports that one of the detainees is the son of an opposition MP.

The United States government often sponsors projects that involve youth and civil society as part of its broader commitment to encourage a range of voices to be heard. These non-partisan and non-violent youth organizations as well as the organizers of the weekend's events intended to engage youth in their civic duty to take part in the political process and raise their voices about issues of concern to them. DRC government officials and ruling coalition parties were invited to the event.

The U.S. government strongly objects to the DRC government's violation of basic freedoms of speech and of peaceful assembly. A troubling trend of the Government of the DRC restricting the freedom of civil society to speak out is emerging and was accentuated by the civil unrest of last January, in which students featured prominently.

Recent events underline the importance of USAID's support for free, fair, credible and timely elections in the DRC through citizen and voter education and citizen participation in elections observation.

Mr. MEADOWS. So let me follow up a little bit further. Your involvement in the democratic process is really not one of trying to influence governments as much as it is trying to make sure that the people in those African countries have a voice to be able to select their own leadership. It is not about setting up governments, is that correct?

Mr. POSTEL. Yes, sir. We are not there to push for specific candidates or specific platforms, but to try to encourage free, fair, transparent processes that get everybody involved and intelligently working through the issues.

Mr. MEADOWS. Well, and I am glad you answered that because I have met with a number of African leaders, Ambassadors, heads of state and I have expressed to them over and over our desire to make sure that we have an open and democratic process. And many of them believe that our influence, your influence, candidly, is there to influence the politics of that particular day. So that is really like nails on a chalkboard because I know that that is not what any of us want to see there. So you are here today. Your testimony is that setting up governments and influencing the outcome is not what it is all about? I think that should be a softball question.

Mr. POSTEL. Definitely not, Congressman.

Mr. MEADOWS. So let me go a step further and this is a message to take back to some in the State Department. When we see reports recently of funds being given to a nonprofit that indirectly, and I don't want to make this political, but when we see funds, $350,000, being filtrated in to affect elections in a democratic country of Israel, and you know what I am talking about, it undermines everything that we are trying to do and what you are trying to do because they take that narrative and say well, if you are willing to influence it there, what is to stop us from influencing it in some African country? Would you agree that that is a problem?

Mr. POSTEL. So——

Mr. MEADOWS. If you were an African leader, let me put it that way, instead of speaking for USAID. Would you believe that that would be a problem?

Mr. POSTEL. I believe that it would be not helpful at all. It would be a problem if some of these heads of state think that somehow we are trying to directly advocate for them or against them as opposed to understanding that we are there about the process and for the sake of free, transparent, open elections. So I will take your message back.

Mr. MEADOWS. And let it be clear, I am here to support you in any way that I possibly can because I believe in the future of what you are trying to do and really the future of the African continent. There is great work to be done there.

At the same time, if the State Department is sending a conflicting message and I have been silent on a lot of this stuff, if they are sending a conflicting message, it creates an integrity problem for me and what I have got to do is make sure that if you take that back and I am saying this in the strongest terms, that it will not be tolerated, using American taxpayer dollars and I want the message to go out to all the African countries. There are many of us here on Capitol Hill that believe the use of American taxpayer money to establish a government of our choosing is not what we do. We want the people of those countries to establish their own leadership. Would you agree with that?

Mr. POSTEL. Yes, sir.

Mr. MEADOWS. Alright. Thank you. And I again thank you for your service and I just feel like those two areas are areas that we need to address. I appreciate the patience of the chair. We are going to be following all the other four panelists back in our office. I apologize, I have got to run and deal with Hezbollah. That is a lot easier than this.

Mr. POSTEL. Thank you, sir.

Mr. MEADOWS. Thank you.

Mr. EMMER. The Chair recognizes Mr. Bera.

Mr. BERA. Thank you, Mr. Chairman. And I want to thank the ranking member. Just to reiterate comments that Africa, for all of its challenges, is a continent full of promise and the work that you are doing, the work of making sure in the short term there are free and fair elections and in the longer term that there is a culture of voting, a culture of peaceful transition is not easy work, but it is necessary work and certainly reflects the values of our great nation.

I would also reiterate what my colleague, Congressman Meadows, suggested that it is not our goal or our business to do anything other than help ensure free and fair elections. In that note, I would be curious, as you look at some of the nations of Africa where USAID and others are engaged in short term in ensuring free and fair elections, what is the culture of voting in many of these nations? Again, we have our own challenges in terms of the culture of voting, but I would be curious what your sense is, just in general terms.

Mr. POSTEL. Thank you for your question. I think there are probably some who are more expert than me, but my general understanding is that it varies across different countries and that in some cases there may be a limited experience with formal voting as we currently experience it here, but there are elements of selection of village elders or other sorts of selection processes that actually have a long history, I believe, in a number of the countries, but it really varies as you would expect.

Mr. BERA. So maybe that as we approach these countries, as opposed to saying well, here is what our culture of voting is and here is how we vote, making sure that we are understanding their culture of voting and how they might interpret that selection process which may be slightly different, but still again if there is a fair and democratic—is that pretty accurate?

Mr. POSTEL. Two things, Congressman. First of all, when we do our work, we always with our partners look at the circumstances in the country. And so as we design the work in partnership with local organizations and government and everybody, we very much try to be sensitive to these differences to make sure, because that is how you help make sure it is effective.

But the other thing I would say is that polling over the last 10, 15 years has shown that the percentage of people who feel very strongly that they want to vote, they want a democracy and their understanding of what that involves is rapidly rising. So in one sense they are coming around and are really interested in the same sort of democracy that we have here.

Mr. BERA. Great. Next question. Who are other partner countries that we are working with? Obviously, France has a long history on the continent and are there other partner countries that we are working with, partner democracies?

Mr. POSTEL. Thank you for your question. There are a bunch. Of course, France and the UK are active in a number of countries, especially their former colonies. The Nordics, Scandinavia, Norway, Sweden, Denmark and so forth, have often worked on elections and civil society and peaceful coexistence issues across Africa and we have partnered with them.

We see several other donors as well, such as the Canadians, the Germans, and others. So there are number of different international donors that work on these things and we are trying very hard to coordinate with them in all cases and in a number of cases, outright partner, and do it together.

Mr. BERA. Another question, again, listening to the questions that Congressman Meadows had asked, you know, I do hear reports of U.S.-based campaign consultants often getting hired to go run campaigns in some of these African nations. I would be curious to get your take. If some of these private sector campaign consultants are coming in, being hired by one candidate or another candidate, clearly with the goal of getting that candidate elected, if that becomes an issue, if others see—they may not always know that. They will see someone who is American and they may kind of blur the line. Are you seeing an increase in kind of these outside private consultants coming in? Does that make your work more difficult?

Mr. POSTEL. I am not too expert in that, Congressman, but I know of some cases where the candidates themselves have hired external consultants who may be out of the U.S. or they could also be out of Europe and other places. You know, that is part of what they do campaigning, but we are sticking to the process. And we work with political parties to make sure that they run themselves in a professional way, but it is not about candidates or platforms or anything like that. And so we are working also on the mechanics of the election. So to that extent when they have consultants talking about what the messages would be or whatever, that is a different area than in which we are working.

Mr. BERA. And I would just for the record want to make sure that is not the policy of the United States Government, although sometimes, again, in the recent elections in Israel, I think there were folks saying well, it is an administration trying to influence an election by having consultants go there again. That is not our policy. Our policy is to ensure free and fair elections.

The last question, as we look at some of the countries that were ravaged with Ebola and so forth, are there unique challenges that again, not knowing exactly what their election timetable is like, things that USAID is thinking about, going forward in terms of helping build some of that infrastructure?

Mr. POSTEL. Thank you for your question, Congressman. You may remember that actually Liberia had an election in December amidst this. It does absolutely make it more complicated because you have people coming in contact and handling things that they are passing to each other where if somebody were infected and in the voting queue or whatever, it could actually lead to transmission; it was widely discussed about how to do this. And our medical and humanitarian experts, I believe, were consulted informally about best practices to try to make sure that that wasn't a problem. And Guinea which has an election coming up, will also have to be attentive to that. So it is a concern as we try to deal with the Ebola problem. And then at the same time, we wouldn't want anybody to have new complications introduced, but on the same token you have got to have elections. It is not an excuse not to have elections.

Mr. BERA. Right. Thank you.

Mr. EMMER. Thank you, Mr. Bera. Mr. Postel, thank you very much for being here today. We appreciate your time and your testimony. And I just as a matter of form want to make it clear that your complete submission will be made part of the record as will the next panel, their complete submissions will be entered into the record as well. I want to thank you for being here today and at this point we will call up the second panel.

As they are moving to the table, why don't we introduce them?

Mr. William Sweeney serves as the president and CEO and IFES. Prior to these positions, he also served as a member of the Board of Directors and was board chairman at IFES. He has a life-long background in democracy promotion and public policy with considerable experience in both the public and private sectors. He was deputy chairman of the Democratic National Committee and executive director of the Democratic Congressional Campaign Committee. He has been an official election observer in the Philippines, Russia, Jamaica, and Nicaragua. Welcome to the panel, Mr. Sweeney.

Ms. Gretchen Birkle currently serves as regional director for Africa, at the International Republican Institute where she is responsible for developing and managing programs in transitioning African countries. She has extensive experience managing democracy and governance programs in closed societies and developing countries around the world. She served as senior coordinator at the State Department's Bureau of Democracy, Human Rights, and Labor where she provided strategic direction for programming and human rights reporting and represented the bureau by testifying before Congress. Ms. Birkle has observed elections in Africa, Asia, Eurasia, and the Middle East.

Mr. Eric Robinson serves as a senior program officer with the Africa Program at the National Endowment for Democracy. In his role, he oversees the East, Horn, and Southern Africa regions and works specifically on Somalia and Eritrea. He also provides oversight to more than 25 NED Core Institute projects in the region. Prior to his appointment at NED, he lived in Puntland, Somalia for 6 months under a U.N. Development Programme consultancy for civil society and he worked for several organizations in the United States implementing federally-funded programs related to refugees, asylees, and civil society development in newcomer communities in the United States.

Mr. Patrick Merloe is senior associate and director of electoral programs at the National Democratic Institute. He has more than 30 years of experience in promoting citizen empowerment, governmental accountability, and public policy advocacy and oversees many of the Institute's programs. Mr. Merloe has participated in more than 150 international missions for NDI to more than 65 countries concentrating on conflict-sensitive states and countries that are vulnerable to authoritarian tendencies and has produced a dozen publications on comparative law, human rights, and elections, and he served as the principal drafter and negotiator of the Declaration of Principles for International Election Observation.

Thanks to everyone on the panel for being here today and we will start with testimony from Mr. William Sweeney.

STATEMENT OF MR. WILLIAM SWEENEY, PRESIDENT AND CHIEF EXECUTIVE ONFFICER, INTERNATIONAL FOUNDATION FOR ELECTORAL SYSTEMS

Mr. SWEENEY. Mr. Chairman, Ranking Member Bass, and distinguished members of the subcommittee, on behalf of the International Foundation for Electoral Systems, I deeply appreciate this opportunity to discuss the impact of U.S. electoral support in sub-Saharan Africa.

Let me start by commending this subcommittee for its constant engagement and focus on all the issues concerning democratic development in Africa. This hearing is another spotlight by the subcommittee, thank you.

Since 1987, the International Foundation for Electoral Systems, better known as IFES, has worked in over 145 countries to support citizens' rights to participate in free, fair, transparent, and accountable elections. Our active programs in Burkina Faso, Burundi, the Central African Republic, Côte d'Ivoire, Guinea, Kenya, Libya, Liberia, Mali, Nigeria, Uganda, and Zimbabwe empower the individuals and institutions that make democracy work at every turn of the electoral cycle.

IFES provides technical assistance to strengthen local capacity and electoral inclusiveness in societies that aspire to realize their full democratic potential.

Mr. Chairman, as we prepare for Nigeria's March 28th election, we should recognize that every Nigerian who votes is choosing the ballot over the bullet. Nigeria has a history of election-related violence. There were violent episodes in 2007 and 2011. Nigerians' vote this time is a personal rejection of Boko Haram, their public threats to this election, and the terrorist legacy since 2009 of 13,000 dead, 1.5 million forced to flee their homes, and kidnappings including the 219 schoolgirls. In the United States, political factions don't kill poll workers and burn down polling stations.

On March 28th, Nigerians will once again courageously exercise their human right to choose the leadership of their country and to vote for stability and democracy. Since taking his post as chairman of the Independent National Electoral Commission or the INEC in late 2010, Chairman Jega has brought a new level of professionalism and integrity to the institution. The introduction of the biometric register, while costly, was seen by many Nigerians as an important step in cutting down on the possibility of voter fraud and ballot stuffing. Since 2010, Chairman Jega has also pioneered internal reorganization of INEC's departments as well as new policies and procedures to improve efficiency and effectiveness of the bureaucracy.

Domestic and international observers commended the INEC for process improvements and their integrity in the conduct of the 2011 elections, a substantial improvement over 2007, according to the Department of State statement. Despite the highly politicized environment surrounding the INEC and the elections in Nigeria, Chairman Jega has managed to maintain a reputation for being impartial and professional and is well respected by Nigerian civil society and citizens. He will finish his term in June 2015.

Let me now briefly summarize our written statement. All the political situations in the countries under discussion are fragile. Public institutions have large mandates with little time to build capacity even if resources are available. None of the electoral management bodies, or EMBs, in these countries have had the luxury of time in office to demonstrate independence from the political tensions and unrest currently underway. However, the elections represent the best of opportunity to peacefully address political disputes and give all parties time to come together as a community and as a nation.

The alternative to the election process and outcome is quite simple and direct. Military or authoritarian rule is hopefully a closing chapter in Africa, but it remains a clear alternative. U.S. assistance to the election process remains critical to supporting the voices and votes of the Africans who have demonstrated a hope for democracy both according to polling data and by their courage to vote.

IFES' focus is the election process conducted by the public institution, the election management body. Much of the cost of an election, personnel, infrastructure, down to ballots and ballot boxes, are part of the public budget of the country. Technical assistance introduces global standards, best practices, strategic planning, and specialized programs for outreach to women, persons with disability, youth, ethnic, indigenous, and religious minorities which are of particular importance in conflict zones.

The challenges in Africa are both immediate, 25 elections are scheduled in the next 21 months, and imminent. Africa has a young population about to come of age and enter their society as adults. The Afrobarometer suggests that young voters will participate, but their expectations are higher and they will then drop out of the process if things do not change.

IFES is proud of its record of partnership in sub-Saharan Africa. We are both honored and grateful for the confidence USAID, the U.S. Department of State, and our international partners have demonstrated in our capacity and commitment through their continued support. Mr. Chairman, and members of the subcommittee, democracy in Africa will certainly be tested in 2015 and beyond. The real tests are ahead of us.

In 2014, there were more South African voters who came of age since Nelson Mandela's first election in 1994 than the rest of the electorate. The rest of the electorate remembered the apartheid era. But that wasn't the majority of voters in South Africa in 2014. The demographic challenge of the next generation—their aspirations and their fears—were made personal to all of us by another investment in their future by the U.S. Congress: The Mandela Washington Fellows attending last summer's U.S.-Africa Leaders Summit.

There are no final victories in politics, or elections, or democracy. The challenges will always be ahead of us. Democracy is not measured in one moment, one election, one success, or one failure. It is an ongoing process, and one that the International Foundation for Electoral Systems is committed to support. Thank you.

[The prepared statement of Mr. Sweeney follows:]

U.S. Election Support in Africa

Testimony of William R. Sweeney, Jr.
President & CEO, International Foundation for Electoral Systems

House Committee on Foreign Affairs
Subcommittee on Africa, Global Health, Global Human Rights,
and International Organizations

March 18, 2015

Testimony of William R. Sweeney, Jr.
President & CEO, International Foundation for Electoral Systems

"U.S. Election Support in Africa"

House Committee on Foreign Affairs
Subcommittee on Africa, Global Health, Global Human Rights,
and International Organizations

March 18, 2015

Mr. Chairman, Ranking Member Karen Bass, and distinguished members of the Subcommittee: on behalf of the International Foundation for Electoral Systems, I deeply appreciate this opportunity to discuss the impact of U.S. electoral support in Sub-Saharan Africa.

Since 1987, the International Foundation for Electoral Systems, better known as IFES, has worked in over 145 countries to support citizens' right to participate in free, fair, transparent and accountable elections. Our active programs in Burkina Faso, Burundi, the Central African Republic, Côte d'Ivoire, Guinea, Kenya, Liberia, Mali, Nigeria, Uganda, and Zimbabwe empower the individuals and institutions that make democracy work at every turn of the electoral cycle. IFES provides technical assistance to strengthen local capacity and electoral inclusiveness in societies that aspire to realize their full democratic potential.

Mr. Chairman, given that American resources and interests are at stake, it is both right and important to examine the effectiveness and efficiency of American electoral assistance in Sub-Saharan Africa. Has U.S. assistance had a positive impact? Are the long term needs of Africa's electoral systems being met? How can assistance, moving forward, be as efficient and effective as possible? What recommendations can implementing organizations share to improve political and electoral processes in Africa?

After all, we are all well aware of the many obstacles to democracy in Africa. The electoral landscape is complex, but I ask you to frame this troubled picture with all of the recent, remarkable triumphs of African democracy, victories in nations like Liberia, Ghana, and Guinea that would have seemed unlikely 10 or twenty years ago: the peaceful transitions we've seen; the millions that are increasingly choosing ballot boxes over coups as a vehicle for change; the fledgling culture of trust emerging from the dust of terrible, violent conflicts.

This is why, Mr. Chairman, the recommendation I respectfully make today is that the U.S. Congress maintain and even increase American engagement with democracy and governance programming, particularly such public institution building as the strengthening of electoral management bodies (EMBs) and electoral cycles. Such support directly aids the institutions and individuals best positioned to promote peaceful change, and arms them with the necessary knowledge to tailor democratic ideals to each unique nation.

Kenya's 2013 elections speak to the progress that can be made when the U.S. Government partners with Africa's public institutions. The Kenyan election of December 27, 2007, resulted in over 1,200 deaths, thousands injured, over 300,000 people displaced and around 42,000 houses and businesses looted or destroyed.[1] After the Kriegler and Waki Commission Reports, the country spent years rebuilding its public institutions to prepare for the 2013 elections. Mr. Chairman, Kenya did not burn on March 4, 2013, and the elections' results were certified by the Kenyan Supreme Court. I would like to believe that investments by USAID, the United Kingdom's Department for International Development, the Canadian Department of Foreign Affairs, Trade and Development and others, as well as the technical support by IFES to Kenya's Independent Electoral and Boundaries Commission, played an important role Kenya's triumph.

Robust support from the U.S. government is critical now, more than ever, as continued U.S. support of elections in Sub-Saharan Africa will incrementally help stabilize emerging democracies and will be the bedrock upon which new democracies are be built. I say "incrementally," as elections are not in themselves change incarnate, but rather a medium for the transition from tyranny to stable representative government. Democracy is not a one-time inoculation against despotism, violence and corruption, but a journey, Mr. Chairman, which our own great country and all other mature democracies took decades, and wars, to muddle through. IFES is proud of the progress being made in Africa, particularly given the cost-effectiveness of our programming: for example, our 18-month program in Burkina Faso is projected to total $1.3 million and our 15-month program in Uganda, $1.15 million. These projects are a drop in the Foreign Assistance bucket, and are none the less producing significant results.

For all of the challenges Africa has and will continue to face, the story of elections in Africa—while still unfinished—is one of success, and one written by and with the African people with the technical support provided by IFES and our partners. IFES is backed by USAID and the U.S. Department of State, as well as global bilateral partners such as the Canadian Department of Foreign Affairs, Trade and Development (DFATD) and the United Nations Development Programme (UNDP), which have also identified the potential for democratic change in Africa.

Introduction: Africa's "Democracy Deficit"

Make no mistake—African citizens endorse democracy. Nearly 87 percent of Sub-Saharan Africa's eligible population is registered to vote; over 45 million ballots were cast in the region in 2014 alone[2]; and a recent Afrobarometer publication based on more than 51,000 face-to-face interviews in 34 countries reveals that the demand for democracy in Africa exceeds supply.[3] This "democracy deficit" felt amongst the vast majority of citizens is not surprising, given the oftentimes predatory political ambitions of the elite. It is

---

[1] "REPORT ON POST-ELECTION VIOLENCE IN KENYA - UN Human Rights Team." Ushahidi RSS. N.p., 20 Mar. 2008. Web. 16 Mar. 2015. <http://www.ushahidi.com/2008/03/20/report-on-post-election-violence-in-kenya-un-human-rights-team/>.

[2] The total number of votes casts in sub-Saharan Africa in 2014, as reported by International IDEA, is 45.134 million. "International IDEA." Voting from Abroad Database. N.p., n.d. Web. 13 Mar. 2015. <http://www.idea.int/elections/vfa/search.cfm>.

[3] "Demand for Democracy Is Rising in Africa, But Most Political Leaders Fail to Deliver", Michael Bratton and Richard Houessou, 23 April 2014 Afrobarometer Policy Paper #11; http://www.afrobarometer.org/files/documents/policy_brief/ab_r5_policypaperno11.pdf

particularly evident in a number of countries, including Cameroon, Côte d'Ivoire, Nigeria, Uganda and Zimbabwe. The survey further found that although less than half (43 percent) consider their country a democracy, they were nonetheless satisfied with the way democracy works. The demand and desire for democracy by the African people also provides hope that the so-called "democracy recession"—as described by various scholars who argue that there is a steady erosion of global levels of democracy and freedom—can and should be countered.

Mr. Chairman, a robust rule of law not only protects the institutional policies and electoral frameworks that provide the foundation for a healthy democracy, but also fosters confidence in the integrity of the electoral process. However, credible elections are only possible if an election management body is constitutionally independent and capable of managing the full electoral cycle. To accomplish this, it must be equipped with qualified leadership, a competent cadre of election officials and support staff, sound election management procedures and an adequate budget. A successfully-managed electoral cycle[4] establishes expectations that the next cycle will yield equal levels of satisfaction and credibility, as well as engenders confidence in the process and acceptance of the outcome. Collectively, these factors strengthen a country's political and constitutional processes and deepen the expectation that regular conduct of elections is the norm—a sentiment that we in the United States are fortunate enough to take for granted.

Two Pan-African Charters define the opportunity for voter enfranchisement to continue to grow. Article 13 of the African Charter on Human and People's Rights provides citizens with "...*the right to participate freely in the government of his country, either directly or through freely chosen representatives in accordance with the provisions of the law*". The African Charter on Democracy, Elections and Governance obliges signatories to "*Nurture, support and consolidate good governance by promoting democratic culture and practice, building and strengthening governance institutions and inculcating political pluralism and tolerance*", as well as to "*Promote the holding of regular free and fair elections to institutionalize legitimate authority of representative government as well as democratic change of governments.*"

In 2015 alone, some 311 million people in Africa are registered to participate in 40 presidential, parliamentary and local government elections, as well as three referenda. The electorates range in size from the island state of São Tomé and Príncipe's 92,000 registered voters to Nigeria's 73 million. The extent to which these voters exercise their franchise is a function of confidence in the democratic process and evidence of their belief in the election management body's institutional integrity. Elections in the Sub-Saharan countries of Burundi, Guinea, Mali and Nigeria will be of particular importance, as they will not only test the countries' commitment to the rule of law, but also the institutional capacity of the respective election management bodies. In addition, elections in Burkina Faso and Côte d'Ivoire will mark the transition from post-conflict governance to democracies.

---

[4] "What Is the Electoral Cycle?" Electoral Cycle —. N.p., n.d. Web. 13 Mar. 2015. <http://aceproject.org/electoral-advice/electoral-assistance/electoral-cycle>.

As partners in the pursuit for credible elections, we are acutely aware that the challenges African nations face are as diverse as the region itself. Mr. Chairman, I am honored to testify today on the significant—but not insurmountable—hurdles African nations face in the pursuit of free, fair, accountable and transparent elections, as well as new, cost-effective opportunities to harness both the power of grassroots engagement and cutting-edge, yet accessible, technology to strengthen election management, mitigate and prevent electoral violence, fortify the integrity and transmission of electoral outcomes, and empower the individuals that make democracy work day-to-day, and election-to-election. IFES takes pride in its unique ability to tailor global best practices in election administration to local needs and provide the tools, training and technical assistance required to carry out credible elections. We envision a world in which every individual has a voice and a vote. The continued support of the U.S. Government—particularly USAID—is imperative to this goal.

Burundi: Harnessing Grassroots and Technology to Mitigate Violence

In June 2015, Burundi has scheduled presidential and parliamentary elections that will test the viability of the country's political institutions. Many analysts fear that incidents of violence will mar the country's 2015 elections. The threat of electoral violence is very real in Burundi, particularly because the concepts of citizen participation in and the selection of leaders through elections have not yet been fully woven into the country's political culture. Regardless of the elections' credibility, electoral violence has the potential to undermine results and spark widespread conflict.

In response to these challenges, IFES has implemented a comprehensive program to encourage reform and provide the tools that can assist local officials in conducting credible and secure elections. In addition to providing technical assistance to the Independent National Electoral Commission (CENI), IFES supports a peaceful electoral process through civic and voter education, as well as through the implementation of Early Warning/Early Response (EWER) technology. EWER works on a grassroots-level to help isolate and deescalate electoral violence by collecting, analyzing, and producing public reports on local instances of violence, as well as providing recommendations to electoral commissions, police, civil society organizations, and community leaders on preventing future incidents. In another promising effort to prevent and monitor electoral conflict, later this month, IFES will launch an open source, *Ushahidi*-based mapping platform for nationwide monitors to report occurrences of electoral violence through mobile communications, and will pair the platform with the implementation of peace committees as a community-based early response measure. These exciting advancements will proactively mitigate the risk of electoral violence and help contain instances of violence that may occur—they may save lives as well as elections, Mr. Chairman, and are worthy of American support.

To complement IFES' efforts to mitigate electoral violence, and as part of its support to and in collaboration with the CENI, IFES has facilitated communication with relevant stakeholders and drafted a proactive work plan to effectively manage the electoral process. In order to encourage an active and informed citizenry, IFES also continues to work with several civil society organizations and radio stations to conduct grassroots civic and voter education sessions that enhance widespread understanding of the electoral process.

The Central African Republic: A Fragile Opportunity for Change

Although the intensity of the civil war between Séléka and anti-Balaka militia in the Central African Republic has subsided, the country remains highly unstable, as starkly illustrated by an almost complete lack of state presence outside the capital, Bangui. Following the cessation of most conflict, an 18-month transitional period overseen by an interim council was established, with the intention of concluding with presidential and legislative elections. However, thousands of ex-Séléka militia are still armed, and maintain significant influence in several of the country's 16 prefectures. This faction has prevented the National Election Authority (ANE) from establishing offices in these regions, going as far as brazenly abducting ANE officials conducting voter education activities. Further, the ANE has opened only 83 of the 141 planned offices as a result of the severe security situation.

Despite some promising developments, including the adoption of a new electoral code, the original February/March 2015 deadline for parliamentary and presidential elections has delayed (by the consensus of the ANE, the Transitional Council, and other stakeholders) to July/August 2015, effectively extending the transitional period to its 24-month maximum. The conduct of these elections is recognized as a central condition to restoring a democratic process in the CAR. However, some key local stakeholders maintain that disarmament is a necessary prerequisite; absent this, many believe the electoral process will likely be derailed. In addition, budgetary limitations, including a nearly 90 percent shortfall, continue to delay election preparations.

Notwithstanding all of these challenges, the international community's short- and long-term support to local stakeholders will eventually yield results. Last fall, when I met with leaders of the ANE, it was very clear that they were aware and entirely transparent about their many difficulties, nonetheless, passionately pled for electoral support. Like citizens in many African nations, they are weary of the power-hungry games played by the elite, and have the courage, resolve and pragmatism to implement democracy—they simply lack the resources.

This is why IFES is proud that since September 2014, through its U.S. Department of State-funded "Electoral Support to the Central African Republic," or ESCAR, program, we have worked with the ANE to provide targeted, rapid-response technical support in the pre-election period via the deployment of high-caliber technical experts. For example, IFES has deployed electoral law and voter registration experts that have developed subsequently-adopted changes to the country's electoral code, as well as a provisional operational plan for the ANE to facilitate an organized and efficient electoral process. The entire budget for this 5 month program (which we expect to be granted a no-cost extension to June 2015) was $297,000.

Several challenges, both political and organizational, lay ahead for elections in the CAR. The transitional government is soon expected to conduct a forum in Bangui on issues of reconciliation, political challenges and next steps on the transition process; the decisions made during these talks will undoubtedly have a significant impact on the election timeline and implementation. Additionally, the details of the voter registration process have yet to be finalized, and a recent decision by the electoral commission to suspend biometric identifiers in registration has sparked confusion on appropriate registration methodology and documentation—particularly with regard to the large internally displaced population and refugees in Chad and Cameroon—which will inevitably affect the efficiency of the electoral process. The elections ultimately have the potential to be credible and transparent, but their success will depend on the ability of the ANE to efficiently and comprehensively manage the registration and polling process amidst political instability.

Burkina Faso: Great Expectations

Burkina Faso's presidential and legislative elections in October 2015 will conclude a precarious 12-month transitional period under a military-civilian government, established after the resignation of former President Blaise Compaoré, which, after his 27 years in office, was widely regarded as a democratic success.

Popular expectations for change are high in the post-Compaoré era, and IFES and its partners are working to fulfill the hopes of Burkinabé citizens. The October 2015 elections offer an unprecedented opportunity to deepen citizens' involvement in electoral and political processes, increase citizens' confidence in the integrity of voting processes and systems and enable young people to channel their new-found activism into peaceful political participation for the first time in over a generation. To capitalize on this environment, and with USAID funding, IFES will conduct a rapid assessment of Burkina Faso's National Independent Electoral Commission's (also known as CENI) needs, so that we may provide targeted technical assistance in support of the upcoming elections. Currently, IFES also plans to work with the CENI to address gaps in key areas such as securing electoral materials, as well as election results tabulation and transmission. In addition, IFES and the CENI will collaborate with local civil society organizations to bolster and disseminate civic and voter education messages that emphasize the need for peaceful elections, especially among youth.

While the Burkinabé population's expectations for transparent and credible elections are high, they are not unrealistic, and are in fact consistent with other Sub-Saharan democracy-deficit countries. However, along with great opportunity, the October elections also carry the potential for great risk. Unless they are viewed as credible, and the results are accepted as a legitimate expression of popular choice, alienated Burkinabé citizens could mobilize as they did so effectively in 2014 to unseat Compaoré.

This popular sentiment lends promise that IFES' key activity in Burkina Faso—assisting the CENI with transparent results tabulation and transmission procedures—will be critical to the public's acceptance of the results and the potential, as well as welcome, return to a popularly-elected democratic government. It is precisely at this juncture when an emerging democracy such as Burkina Faso is most in need of continued support from the United States and organizations such as IFES, to allow the potential for peaceful political change to occur, and for the seeds of democracy to take root.

Mali: After Turmoil, Democracy

Although the deployment of nearly 10,000 U.N. peacekeepers to Mali is credited with permitting the presidential elections of 2013 due to continued insecurity, voter rolls could not be accurately updated and the presidential and local elections scheduled for April 2015 have been delayed until October 2015.

With funding from USAID, IFES provided technical assistance for the 2013 transitional elections to all three electoral management bodies in Mali, with an emphasis on support to the Ministry of Territorial Administration. Included in this support were assistance with results tabulation and transmission and poll worker training.

Under a newly USAID-funded program, IFES is strengthening the capacity of Mali's National Independent Electoral Commission (CENI) through poll worker trainings in Bamako's six communes, with a goal of reaching an estimated 10,860 poll workers. These trainings are "cascade-style," meaning we teach individuals to train others in their community to become poll workers. By embracing this efficient, cost-effective, and sustainable model, IFES has successfully trained over 1 million poll workers worldwide. Likewise, IFES is developing an elections supervision platform, and anticipates supporting the electoral reform process by organizing a workshop that would include participants from the Government of Mali and the three election management bodies to discuss the results of their studies of the changes to the legal framework.

Côte d'Ivoire: A Vital Post-Conflict Milestone

With funding provided by USAID, IFES is conducting an assessment of the Ivoirian legal and regulatory framework governing elections in anticipation of the November 2015 presidential elections, which represent a crucial post-conflict milestone as well as an enormous test for the country's Independent Electoral Commission (CEI). Specific areas under review include voter registration, boundary delimitation, electoral campaigning, political finance regulations, electoral dispute management, and the compilation and publication of results. The analysis will provide a comprehensive list of recommended reforms and used as a basis for inclusive discussions between stakeholders.

In addition, IFES is undertaking a strategic planning exercise with the CEI to outline roles and responsibilities and clarify election administration and operations procedures. One of the global best practices of the IFES Strategic Planning tools is the engagement by election commissions with all electoral stakeholders: parties, candidates, civil society, religious leaders, media; with a particular emphasis on the inclusion of women, indigenous populations, and persons with disabilities. IFES will also deploy an Election Integrity Specialist to train Commissioners on the development and implementation of robust fraud and malpractice control procedures.

Because scars from the 2010 post-election violence are still relatively fresh, IFES is also conducting a Conflict Sensitivity Analysis in order to better understand the actors, causes, history, dynamics and direction of conflict in Côte d'Ivoire—especially in the realm of political dialogue and the holding of national-level elections in 2015 and 2016. As IFES programming is not limited to specific electoral events, but rather on the entire electoral cycle, activities in Côte d'Ivoire will include milestones and anticipated timelines through the 2018 elections.

Conclusion: Heeding the Voices of Change

Mr. Chairman, the electoral process in multiple Sub-Saharan countries is threatened by a plethora of factors. Among the most ominous are insurgencies and violent conflicts causing mass internal displacement in countries where the state is unable to convincingly restore order—CAR, Nigeria, and Mali—and the potential for post-election violence in Côte d'Ivoire, Nigeria and Burundi. In other instances, violence can erupt from an election result, as evidenced by Burundi and Côte d'Ivoire. Although the electoral process itself is not always a direct target, in some instances it is the clear target. In Nigeria, for example, Boko Haram's continued public threats to disrupt the February 2015 elections resulted in a six-week postponement.

Advancements in election technology are allowing for greater enfranchisement, especially among such traditionally marginalized groups as women, persons with disabilities, and ethnic and religious minorities. Biometric voter registration and voter identification systems used in Kenya and Nigeria are more sophisticated and capture more information than any system deployed in the United States. These technologies have the capability of reducing ballot-stuffing and voter misidentification, and even mitigating the possibility of post-election violence resulting from allegations of vote tally manipulation. When the appropriate technology is identified and properly deployed, these emerging tools have the potential of engraining new democratic norms where they are absent, and permanently establishing national trust in the conduct and outcome of elections.

Empirical data from the Afrobarometer survey demonstrate the strong desire among Sub-Saharan countries for democratic governance through elections. In Liberia, for example, although the Ebola outbreak that ravaged the country in 2014 instilled such fear that the elections were postponed, the country's determination to hold the constitutionally-mandated elections was unwavering. With IFES' technical and material support, Liberia's National Elections Commission conducted a nearly flawless election under unprecedented conditions. Having only recently emerged from the rule of Charles Taylor and a devastating civil war, Liberia's progress in election management is remarkable. Liberia had 10 years of civil war. President Ellen Johnson-Sirleaf is in her second term and the country is already preparing for the next presidential election in 2017, in which Ms. Johnson-Sirleaf will not be running per the constitutionally-mandated term limits.

The quality of elections not only embodies the integrity of the democratic process and the rule of law, but also creates expectations that transparent and free elections should be the norm, not the exception. It is therefore imperative that continued technical and material support be provided to those countries that seek to engrain these practices in their political cultures until they are able to fully manage the process independently. Looking forward to 2016, there are a number of pivotal Sub-Saharan countries that will have the opportunity to further establish democratic norms through elections, including: Uganda (President and National Assembly), Benin (President), Djibouti (President), Chad (President), Democratic Republic of the Congo (President and National Assembly), and Côte d'Ivoire (National Assembly), among others.

IFES is proud of its record of partnership in Sub-Saharan Africa. We are both honored and grateful for the confidence USAID, the U.S. Department of State and our international partners have demonstrated in our capacity and commitment through their continued support. Mr. Chairman, and members of the Subcommittee, democracy in Africa will certainly be tested in 2015 and beyond. The real tests are ahead of us. In 2014, there were more South African voters who came of age since Nelson Mandela's first election in 1994 than remembered the apartheid era. This demographic challenge of the next generation—their aspirations and their fears—were made personal to all of us by another investment in their future by the U.S. Congress: the Mandela Washington Fellows attending last summer's U.S.-Africa Leaders Summit.

There are no final victories in politics, or elections, or democracy. The challenges will always be ahead of us. Democracy is not measured in one moment, one election, one success, or one failure—it is an ongoing process, and one that the International Foundation for Electoral Systems is committed to support. Thank you.

Global Expertise. Local Solutions.
Sustainable Democracy

IFES | 1850 K Street, NW | Fifth Floor | Washington, D.C. 20006 | www.IFES.org

Mr. EMMER. Thank you, Mr. Sweeney.
Ms. Birkle.

STATEMENT OF MS. GRETCHEN BIRKLE, REGIONAL DIRECTOR FOR AFRICA, INTERNATIONAL REPUBLICAN INSTITUTE

Ms. BIRKLE. Thank you, Mr. Chairman, Ranking Member Bass, and members of the subcommittee. Thank you for this opportunity to testify on election support in Africa. Given how many Africans will head to the polls in 2015 and over the next several years, preparing is extremely timely. The International Republic Institute in Africa works to encourage democracy in places where it is absent, help democracy become more effective where it is in danger, and share best practices where democracy is flourishing.

While there are best practices that can serve as models for other countries, there are also broader challenges that could hinder elections in Africa. I would like to highlight four of those broader challenges today. Many African states have made steady progress toward developing and consolidating democracy following centuries of colonialism and underdevelopment, yet, genuine multi-party democracy has yet to take root in most countries and this is the first challenge to highlight as we look at elections in these countries.

The limited capacity of political parties to govern, that is, to exercise legitimate authority and provide basic services to citizens is contributing to increasing citizen distrust and apathy, low voter turnout, and a failure of expectations of democracy among many Africans throughout the continent.

A second challenge is the pervasive trend to attempt to change the rules of the game. Specifically, there are increasing attempts to change laws and yes, even constitutions, to evade term limits. Once in power, leaders often have no desire to foster peaceful, political transitions and instead openly work to change the rules to stay in power. These attempts to change the rules of the game have not gone unnoticed by the people of Africa. Citizens are now protesting against incumbents who are seeking to extend their term in office and unfortunately, these protests often turn violent like we saw last October in Burkina Faso.

What happened in Burkina Faso has had a significant impact on the region and citizens in each country are keeping an eye on their neighbors. As an opposition Member of Parliament from Kinshasa recently told me here in Washington, DC, people in Burundi have seen how the Congolese stood up and the Congolese saw how the people in Burkina Faso stood up. The upcoming elections in DRC are important not only for DRC, but for all of Africa. This underscores the critical need to look at elections and the challenges impacting them along regional lines and not only in isolation for each country.

A third challenge that could impact the outcome of elections in Africa is the huge youth demographic on the continent. The region has the youngest population in the world with two-thirds of its 1 billion population under the age of 25 and half of the population under the age of 19. This means that for many youth, elections set to occur over the next few years will present the first opportunity for them to exercise their right to vote. Tapping into the voices and desires of young people is a challenge for the region, but one that holds extraordinary potential for ushering in new leaders with new ideas. African nations must find ways to engage their growing youth populations to participate positively in the electoral process and help shape the future trajectory of their individual countries and the region as a whole.

The fourth challenge is the potential for electoral violence and ongoing civil conflict. 2015 will be a year of contentious politics where preexisting tensions will intersect with elections. There is an urgency to devise strategies now to prevent and manage electoral violence. This is critical since recurring electoral violence may cause citizens to lose faith in democratization.

Now looking forward, it is imperative to view elections as a process, not a single event. Continued support is needed between elections in order to see sustainable progress. For example, now is the critical time to support aid efforts to encourage broad-based and inclusive strategies for mobilizing voters, particularly marginalized populations such as youth. Citizen engagement and conflict prevention efforts are important and are complemented by polling and programs that encourage political parties and candidates to campaign on policy issues, rather than personalities.

Ultimately, the challenges Africa faces, leaders evading term limits, marginalization of youth, ongoing civil conflicts and potential for election-related violence, are all related to the lack of strong multi-party democratic systems. Once nations fully embrace and adopt competitive, representative, political processes with all of its checks and balances, then these challenges will be better addressed. We should support Africans and their pursuit of prosperity with sustainable democratic institutions and processes where all individuals have the opportunity and incentive to participate in the political process. And where peaceful, political transitions can occur, the people of Africa will be freer to pursue their political and economic aspirations. Thank you.

[The prepared statement of Ms. Birkle follows:]

Congressional Testimony

U.S. Election Support in Africa

Testimony of Gretchen Birkle
Regional Director for Africa
International Republican Institute

U.S. House Committee on Foreign Affairs
Subcommittee on Africa, Global Health, Global Human Rights, and
International Organizations

March 18, 2015

Introduction

Chairman Smith, Ranking Member Bass and Members of the House Committee on Foreign Affairs, Subcommittee on Africa, Global Health, Global Human Rights, and International Organizations, thank you for this opportunity to testify on election support in Africa. Given how many Africans throughout the region will head to the polls in 2015 and over the next several years, this hearing is extremely timely. Some 30 countries have elections between now and the end of 2016. These countries face many challenges, not least of which are attempts among many leaders to evade term limits, the marginalization of youth and ongoing civil conflicts, all of which can exacerbate the potential for violence, before, during and after the upcoming elections. It is critical that the United States and its partners work together to support the African people in their pursuit of democracy, recognizing that elections are only one part of the process.

IRI Africa Programs

The International Republican Institute (IRI) is a nonprofit, nonpartisan organization and one of the four core institutes of the National Endowment for Democracy. Our mission is to encourage democracy in places where it is absent, help democracy become more effective where it is in danger and share best practices where democracy is flourishing. Specifically in Sub-Saharan African, IRI focuses on six core components: bolstering the capacity of multi-party political systems, promoting democratic governance, empowering marginalized groups, legislative institution building, supporting civil society initiatives and strengthening electoral processes. We currently work in Burundi, Cote d'Ivoire, Democratic Republic of the Congo, Kenya, Mali, Niger, Nigeria, Rwanda, South Africa, Tanzania, Uganda and Zimbabwe.

Trends and Challenges in Upcoming Elections

It is valuable that we look at elections across the continent as a whole. While there are best practices that can serve as models for other countries, there are also broader challenges that could hinder elections in Africa and that should be considered as we explore ways to support the electoral process in transitioning African countries. I will highlight four of those broader challenges today.

Lack of multi-party democracy

Many African states have made steady progress toward developing and consolidating democracy following centuries of colonialism and underdevelopment. Since the 'third wave' of transitions through the ballot box, a wave of popular demand and international pressure for political reforms led to the overthrow of numerous authoritarian regimes, single-party dictators and military elites. Yet, genuine multi-party democracy has yet to take root in most countries, and this is the first challenge to highlight as we look at elections in Africa. Without a vibrant political system in place, elections too easily can become a rubber stamp for the party in power. There are many reasons for this absence of multiparty democracy on the continent. Parties are too often personality driven and have ill-defined structures that contribute to inadequate capacity and inefficiency. Even in countries with more competitive politics, the lack of effective political competition has often resulted in unstable and fractured government coalitions that prevent effective governance and offer little inspiration to the voter. Furthermore, many political parties remain ill-equipped to address their countries' immense challenges, particularly staggering inequality and extreme poverty. The limited capacity of political parties to govern – that is, to exercise legitimate authority and provide basic services to citizens – is contributing to increasing citizen distrust and apathy, low voter turnout and a failure of expectations of democracy among many Africans throughout the continent.

Changing the rules

A second challenge is the pervasive trend to attempt to change the rules of the game. Specifically, there are increasing attempts to change laws and even constitutions to evade term limits. Across Africa, the 'politics of personality' continues to present a challenge to democratic transitions and consolidation. Once in power, leaders often have no desire to foster peaceful political transitions and instead openly work to change the rules to stay in power.

Togo is such a country, having abolished presidential term limits from its constitution in 2002. Critics and the opposition have not been able to persuade the ruling Union for the Republic (UNIR) party to support a two-term presidential term limit and talks in the National Assembly to change the constitution broke down in January of this year. Togolese President Faure Gnassingbé has already served two-elected terms in office after he was installed in a military coup upon the 2005 death of his father, who himself had ruled Togo since he took power in 1967. Ignoring the calls of the opposition and international leaders who have warned against African leaders 'who cling to power,' President Gnassingbé accepted the nomination of the UNIR to seek a third term in Togo's April elections.

In Uganda, ironically when multi-party politics was reinstated in 2005, legislation was also passed that year that removed presidential term limits. This has allowed President Museveni to remain in power for nearly 30 years. According to IRI's most recent public opinion poll in Uganda, of 2,402 Ugandans surveyed, 65 percent believe the constitution should limit the president to serve a maximum of two terms. Despite this, President Museveni has already been declared the candidate for his ruling party, the National Resistance Movement, in advance of Uganda's 2016 elections.

Even in countries that have presidential term limits, many leaders continue to seek creative ways to try to circumvent these limits. For instance, in Burundi, where parliamentary and presidential elections are expected to take place in May and June of this year, President Nkurunziza's spokesperson announced on February 15 that the president plans to run for a third term, in direct contradiction to the Arusha Agreement, the 2000 ceasefire accord that established the power-sharing transitional government in the midst of the country's civil war. This effort is despite a failed attempt to change the constitution to permit a third term, which fell one vote short of the 80 percent parliamentary majority needed to amend the constitution. Nkurunziza claims that since he was appointed by parliament for his first term in 2005, he should be able to contest once more. Should Nkurunziza win reelection this spring, which many anticipate he will, it would present Burundi with the dilemma of a president in office for three terms, in direct contradiction to the constitution.

These sort of actions are widespread across the region. Just recently, President Denis Sassou Nguesso's ruling Congolese Worker's Party called for a constitutional change to remove the Republic of Congo's two-term presidential limit and age restriction that excludes candidates more than 70 years old from running for office. The 2002 constitution as it stands now would rule out President Nguesso, who is 71, came into power in 1997 and remained in office through disputed elections in 2002 and 2009.

These attempts to change the rules of the game have not gone unnoticed by the people of Africa. Citizens are protesting against incumbents who are seeking to extend their terms in office, and, unfortunately, these protests often turn violent. Last October, Burkina Faso saw massive demonstrations and widespread protests in response to President Blaise Compaore's attempt to remove presidential term limits. These protests culminated in protestors setting fire to the country's parliament building to prevent a vote on the issue and ultimately resulted in Compaore's fleeing from the country and resigning. The country has since been run by a transitional government with new elections now scheduled for October 2015.

What happened in Burkina Faso has had a significant impact on the region. In the Democratic Republic of Congo (DRC), a provision initially included in the electoral law currently being considered before the Senate required a national census to be conducted prior to the presidential election. This provision would have effectively postponed the next round of elections to 2018 despite the fact that President Kabila's second term is set to expire at the end of 2016. On January 19 and 20, citizens went to the street in the capital Kinshasa and two other towns in protests that quickly turned violent. Human Rights Watch reported some 42 people were killed. As a result of this street action, the Senate removed the controversial clause from DRC's electoral law, and while the census can no longer be used as a delaying tactic, the verdict is still out on whether President Kabila will leave office when his term expires.

What happened in the DRC is particularly relevant for the entire region, and citizens in each country are keeping an eye on their neighbors. As an opposition Member of Parliament from Kinshasa recently said in Washington, D.C., "People in Burundi have seen how the Congolese stood up, and the Congolese saw how people in Burkina Faso stood up. The upcoming elections in DRC are important not only for DRC, but for all of Africa." This underscores the critical need to look at elections and the challenges impacting them along regional lines and not only in isolation for each country.

Marginalization of youth

A third challenge that could impact the outcome of elections in Africa is the huge youth demographic on the continent. The region has the youngest population in the world, with two thirds of its 1 billion population under the age of 25 and half of the population under the age of 19, according to the 2014 United Nations African Economic Outlook report. This means that for many youth, elections set to occur over the next few years will present the first opportunity for them to exercise their right to vote. Furthermore, young people bear a disproportionate burden of the high unemployment rates that many African nations are experiencing. According to the World Bank, youth account for 60 percent of all African unemployed and these statistics fail to encompass those who are underemployed in the informal sector.

It is not surprising, given extreme poverty and unemployment, that youth participation and engagement in political and electoral processes remain relatively low and varies across the region. While Kenya saw more than half a million youth join a *bunge* or community parliament to monitor the 2013 elections, in South Africa, only 22 percent of 18 and 19-year-olds were registered to vote in advance of the May 2014 election, according to the South Africa Independent Electoral Commission. According to a recent Pew Research Center study, young people throughout the developing world, including Africa, are significantly less likely to vote than older people. The study also shows that young people are interested in issues, and that they do want to participate in other forms of activism, for example, by discussing politics online and through social media. They are just less likely to actually go to the polls and vote.

The Pew study underscored the close link between political efficacy and political engagement, whereby people who more strongly believe that they can have an influence on political matters are more likely to participate in political processes than those who lack faith in the process. For the countries surveyed in Africa, roughly two in three people believe that the government does not care about citizen opinion. This is a damaging statistic and could signal low turnout among Africans of all ages during the upcoming elections. If people believe what they think does not matter, how likely will they be to go to polls as a means of expressing their opinions?

Tapping into the voices and desires of young people is a huge challenge for the region, one that holds extraordinary potential for ushering in new leaders with new ideas. African nations must find ways to engage their growing youth populations to participate positively in the electoral process and help shape the future trajectory of their individual countries and the region as a whole.

Civil conflict and electoral violence

Fourth, of the roughly dozen African nations holding elections this year, many are engaged in civil conflicts or are battling terrorism and domestic insurgencies at home. Many also have a history of electoral violence that raises reasons for concern. For the continent, 2015 will be a year of contentious politics where pre-existing tensions will intersect with elections. There is an urgency to devise strategies to prevent and manage electoral violence.

Internal conflicts have already caused the postponement of some elections. Nigeria's February 14 elections were postponed to March 28, according to the Nigerian government, to allow a six-week offensive against Boko Haram to play out. According to Human Rights Watch, there were more than 100 documented Boko Haram attacks in 2014 that claimed the lives of more than 2,500 Nigerians, and we know that hundreds more have been killed so far this year. Separate from the threat of Boko Haram, Nigeria has a history of violence around elections. Upon the announcement of the results of the 2011 presidential election, violence erupted in several Northern states, ultimately killing more than 1,000 people. To date, it has been encouraging to see that promises of nonviolence agreed to in the Abuja Accord, signed by President Goodluck Jonathan, General Mohammadu Buhari and 12 other presidential candidates on January 10, have held firm. IRI is now working at the state level to encourage wider endorsement of the Abuja Accord by local level party officials and activists. Nonetheless, given that the March 28 elections will be the most contested in Nigeria's history, the possibility of violence cannot be dismissed.

Ongoing conflict also contributed toward the postponement of the presidential election in the Central African Republic (CAR). The presidential election in CAR was originally scheduled for February and has since been postponed to August, with calls for even longer delays to allow time for disarmament of the warring militias before elections take place to help deter election-related violence. Similarly, South Sudan's first election since independence in 2011 was initially planned for June 2015, and is now postponed to 2017 as a result of the civil conflict there. Recently, Mali's scheduled local elections for April 2015 have also been postponed to late 2015. Though no official reason for the postponement was given by the government, it is widely believed that insecurity in the northern part of the country contributed to the decision to delay the elections.

Sudan remains entangled in a long-running conflict with rebels in the west in Darfur and the south in South Kordofan and Blue Nile. In December, opposition forces came together under the "Sudan Call," a new political agreement calling for peaceful and popular democratic reform in the country. This agreement was deemed an act of treason by the government and some of its signatories were subsequently arrested. Meanwhile, most opposition groups have refused to participate in the national dialogue initiative launched by President Bashir in 2014 and the National Consensus Forces (the main opposition coalition in Sudan) has called for a boycott of the April 2015 elections. There appears to be a confluence of factors that could tip the scale toward violence.

Other countries have a history of electoral-related violence and some fear a reoccurrence. While countries such as Cote d'Ivoire and Nigeria experienced widespread electoral violence in the past, what is more common is low-intensity violence coupled with voter and candidate intimidation that such countries as the DRC, Uganda and Guinea have witnessed. Elections often risk intensifying existing rivalries and exacerbating societal divisions. This is especially true in countries where basic electoral procedures have been adopted but democratic norms have not yet taken root. For instance, one-party or dominant party systems that characterized many African nations often lead to exclusionary politics where the stakes are high and elections are viewed as a zero-sum game, raising the risk of electoral violence. Not only should more be done to mitigate election-related conflict for the sake of avoiding bloodshed, but it is also critical since recurring electoral violence may cause citizens to lose faith in democratization.

Looking Forward

While it is encouraging that elections have become a regular occurrence in Sub-Saharan Africa, they are still imperfect and much remains to be done to ensure that elections are free, fair, inclusive and transparent throughout the region. Elections are a process, not a single event. United States policymakers and development organizations should continue to provide support throughout the process and not only in the few months leading up to Election Day. The democratic process does not end after the polls are closed. Continued support is needed between elections in order to see sustainable progress. There are steps the United States and its partners can take to help support electoral processes throughout Africa, many of which are relevant even for those elections scheduled later this year.

Because of the resistance among many leaders throughout the region to step aside when their terms expire, it would be helpful to encourage more dialogue on next steps leaders could take once out of office. This is a complicated issue, and there are a variety of reasons that are keeping leaders in office, including fears of being held accountable or made a political target for alleged crimes, such as personal enrichment. The United States and its international partners could coordinate messaging to these leaders to help encourage their peaceful departure and promote a transfer of power that can occur without conflict or bloodshed.

The United States should continue to support important efforts on the ground to bolster democratic activists throughout the region. Now is the critical time to support aid efforts that encourage broad-based and inclusive strategies for mobilizing voters, particularly marginalized populations such as youth. Recurring electoral violence usually signals underlying grievances which is why promoting citizen participation throughout the electoral cycle is critical. Citizens need to find alternative, non-violent ways to air grievances, not just when election results are announced, but in between elections as well. These citizen engagement and conflict-prevention efforts are complemented by polling and programs that encourage political parties and candidates to campaign on policy issues rather than personalities and by programs that educate citizens on these issues to promote an informed, active electorate.

Another important way to strengthen democratic processes throughout Africa is to enhance support for both international and domestic election monitoring to help confirm legitimacy to the electoral process. An important element of election observations is conducting assessment missions in advance of elections to let the country's government and candidates know that the international community is watching and paying attention to the process. In January, IRI conducted such an assessment jointly with the National Democratic Institute in advance of Nigeria's election. The assessment provided an important review of the current political and electoral environment and preparations. It also provided a set of recommendations to enhance citizen confidence in the process, help mitigate violence and demonstrate international support for Nigeria's democratization process. Such assessments can provide guidance for governments, election commission, political parties and citizen groups, as they prepare for national polls.

Ultimately, the challenges Africa faces – leaders evading term limits, marginalization of youth, ongoing civil conflicts and potential for election-related violence – are all related to the lack of strong multi-party democratic systems. Once nations fully embrace and adopt competitive, transparent, representative political processes with all of its checks and balances, then these challenges will be better addressed. We should support Africans in their pursuit of prosperity with sustainable democratic institutions and processes where all individuals have the opportunity and incentive to participate in the political process. And where peaceful political transitions can occur, the people of Africa will be freer to pursue their civil, political, economic, social and cultural aspirations.

Mr. EMMER. Thank you, Ms. Birkle.
Mr. Robinson.

STATEMENT OF MR. ERIC ROBINSON, SENIOR PROGRAM OFFICER FOR EAST AND HORN OF AFRICA, NATIONAL ENDOWMENT FOR DEMOCRACY

Mr. ROBINSON. Mr. Chairman, ranking member, members of the committee, I am honored to speak before your subcommittee regarding the National Endowment for Democracy's support for elections in Africa.

NED began funding civil society organizations working on elections in Africa 25 years ago when we made the first such grant to an organization called GERDDES to monitor the historic elections in Benin in 1990. Last year, NED made nearly 250 grants in Africa and as many as half of these supported election processes in some way. Since the critical role of elections in Africa has already been recognized, I will focus on how NED engages in Africa on elections.

Elections are a necessary, but not sufficient, condition for democracy. Concerning elections, NED supports NGOs that provide civic education, monitor rights violations, and provide forums for citizens to express their views. Currently, many African leaders have attempted to change the constitution to enable them to run for more than two terms, and civil society groups have raised the alarm. This was most recently so in the case of DRC which is NED's largest program in Africa. Most of our nearly 50 partners in DRC have focused on the current political process including elections later this year and next year.

Elections give citizens and institutions practice, knowledge, and familiarity with democratic culture. Even flawed elections can provide space for civil society to conduct civic education. And in relatively closed political environments such as Sudan, Chad, Rwanda, or Ethiopia, NED is supporting civic groups that work in a limited space with the aim of expanding it and laying the foundation for a future democratic dispensation. Elections are not a 1-day event. NED supports domestic observation groups that may follow the process for months or years beforehand. Our grantees have advised electoral commissions, observed and supported voter registration, audited voter lists, monitored media, and organized debates and voter forums.

Elections can serve as a means of conflict resolution, but they can also lead to violence. Therefore, we have supported groups promoting peace and resolving conflict, often in the context of elections. Through CIPE, NED supported the Kenya Association of Manufacturers which played a role in ending the violence after the 2007 elections. Currently in Nigeria, we have grantees that train citizens in the north on conflict resolution and the women's organization promoting Christian-Muslim dialogue. These are but a few examples.

Africa is the world's youngest continent and as demonstrated in Senegal and Burkina Faso last year, youth are moving to the front line of political change whether through elections or popular uprising. In partnership with the World Movement for Democracy, just last weekend NED brought together nearly 100 young democratic activists from across Africa to share experiences and information regarding these transitions. NED's partners engage youth in election processes, pointing them in a positive, democratic direction.

Women have been politically marginalized in much of Africa, but when given the chance have provided tremendous leadership in civil society and government. NED is supporting IRI and NDI to cultivate women's political leadership and the Solidarity Center is working with women to expand their role within unions and labor associations in Africa. With NED funds, the Nigerian Federation of Women produced television programs promoting women's participation in these upcoming elections. In Somaliland, women and youth organizations provided nearly all the monitors for their successful elections. And in Uganda, CEWIGO has had success in cultivating a new generation of female politicians.

We have often seen in Africa that today's democratic champion can become tomorrow's despot, so we don't pick a winner. NED respects pluralism and the political process in support of free and fair elections. Normally, party training is not conducted within 30 days of an election. Funds may not support the candidacy of candidates for public office, and by and large, whatever political loyalties our partners may have, their programs are nonpartisan.

And the politics of the belly still rules much of Africa, meaning that political office often affords the best opportunity for securing material wealth through patronage. NED has supported groups conducting investigative reporting and campaigns against corruption. Our partners help citizens understand that elected officials are their representatives, not their patrons, and that they should not sell their vote for a bag of rice as NAYMOTE, a long-time Liberian grantee, successfully campaigned.

Africans want elections. Even if citizens in some countries are apprehensive about election violence, corruption and impunity have caused apathy. NED's partners support participation and mobilization and those who have observed elections in Africa can testify to the commitment and enthusiasm of voters who may stand in line for hours.

Elections and democracy may still be a work in progress in Africa. We and our grantees are optimistic about the future.

Mr. Chairman, ranking member, and members of the committee, I look forward to your questions.

[The prepared statement of Mr. Robinson follows:]

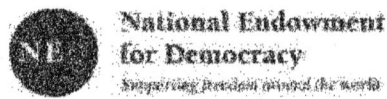

National Endowment for Democracy
Supporting freedom around the world

1025 F Street, NW | Suite 800 | Washington, DC 20004-1409
(202) 378-9700 | (202) 378-9407 fax | E-mail info@ned.org | www.ned.org

U.S. Election Support in Africa

House Committee on Foreign Affairs
Subcommittee on Africa, Global Health, Global Human Rights,
and International Organizations
March 18, 2015

Testimony by

Eric J. Robinson
Senior Program Officer-East, Horn and Southern Africa
National Endowment for Democracy

Mr. Chairman, Ranking Member, Members of the committee, I am honored to speak before your committee on the National Endowment for Democracy's support for elections in Africa. NED began funding civil society organizations working on elections in Africa 25 years ago, when we made the first such grant to an organization called GERDDES to monitor the historic elections in Benin in 1990. Since then, NED has supported hundreds of groups engaged in a broad range of activities that have contributed to election processes. Last year NED made nearly 250 grants in Africa, averaging about $40,000 each, to mostly indigenous civil society organizations. Perhaps as many as half of these were supporting election processes in some way. We have learned some lessons and identified some trends over the years and would like to offer ten points for the committee's consideration.

First, we know that elections are a necessary but not sufficient condition for democracy. No country can claim to be a democracy if it does not hold elections, but we have many examples of countries that hold elections, and that are not democratic. In other words, there must be an "enabling environment." Democracy requires freedom of speech and assembly, freedom of association, and the rule of law, among other conditions. Thus, in the context of elections, NED has supported many NGOs providing civic education, monitoring human rights violations, raising policy issues, and providing forums for citizens to express their views. Strong institutions such as independent courts and electoral commissions are also important, which our partners will also often work with. Elections can be vitally important for determining a country's political trajectory; they spark public interest in government, and should therefore be as inclusive and participatory as possible. Elections in Africa have tended to get better over time, according to the political scientist Steffan Lindborg, giving citizens and institutions practice, knowledge, and familiarity with democratic culture. Elections thus create a virtuous circle that reinforces the free press, civic organizations, accountability, political competition, and other democratic values.

Second, elections are not simply a one-day event, they are a process. The campaign period and the aftermath of the election are also critical. Election Day itself may appear to be peaceful and well-organized, but if the opposition has been sufficiently undermined beforehand or the rigging has been well-engineered, then the elections cannot be said to be free and fair. Thus, NED supports domestic observation groups that may follow the process for months and even years beforehand. Currently many African leaders have attempted to change the constitution to enable them to run for more than two terms, and civil society groups have raised the alarm. This was most recently so in the case of DRC, which is NED's largest program in Africa. Most of our nearly 50 partners in DRC are focused on the current political process, including elections later this year and next year. NED grantees in the DRC and other countries have assisted and advised the electoral commission, observed and supported voter registration, audited the voters list, monitored media coverage, conducted opinion polling, assessed adherence to campaign promises, organized debates between candidates, and held voter forums. Many groups are making use of social media, as well as radio and television, to encourage participation.

Third, elections usually serve as a means of conflict resolution, as was demonstrated most dramatically in South Africa in 1994, but we have learned all too well that elections can also lead to violence. For this reason, we have also supported many groups promoting peace and resolving conflict, often in the context of elections. Through CIPE, for example, NED supported the Kenya Association of Manufacturers, which was instrumental in ending the violence following the 2007 elections. In Zimbabwe, NED supported many groups successfully advocating for peaceful elections two years ago. Currently in Nigeria, NED has made grants to groups such as SEMA to train citizens in the north on conflict resolution, a women's organization promoting Christian-Muslim dialogue, and the Fund for Peace to monitor and map violence, among many others. NED's partners in Cote d'Ivoire have buttressed the fragile reconciliation process in the run-up to elections later this year. Likewise in Burundi, various NED partners are promoting peaceful elections, training journalists to avoid incitement or hate speech, and bringing opposing political activists together to debate peacefully.

Fourth, even flawed elections can provide space for civil society organizations to conduct civic education and raise policy issues. Governments may feel compelled to allow such activity to lend at least a veneer of legitimacy to the process. Even in relatively closed systems such as Sudan, Chad, Rwanda or Ethiopia, NED is supporting civic groups that can take advantage of what space exists and gradually expand it, educate citizens about their rights, and lay the foundations for a future democratic dispensation. Such programs need not legitimize a flawed process, as long as democratic forces have chosen to participate. In Rwanda last year, a NED partner conducted virtually the only international observations of the national elections that were held there. During Sudan's 2010 elections, NED partners composed the domestic observation coalitions that made considerable headway in expanding political rights. In Cameroon, a NED partner is pressing for freedom of assembly, despite restrictions on political party activity caused by new anti-terrorism legislation.

Fifth, engage youth. Africa is the world's youngest continent, and as events in Senegal and Burkina Faso demonstrated last year, they are moving to the frontline of political change, whether through elections or popular uprisings. In partnership with the World Movement for Democracy, just last weekend NED brought together nearly 100 young democratic activists from across Africa to share lessons and experiences regarding these transitions. Youth are impatient; they have the energy; increasingly, they have nothing to lose. NED's partners are pointing youth in a democratic direction, instead of a life of crime, apathy, or Boko Haram. In Nigeria, YIAGA is helping the electoral commission test its new computerized election equipment; and YOSPIS, Youngstars, and the YMCA are encouraging youth participation. In Uganda, the Students for Democracy and UYONET are working to persuade youth not to follow the corrupt electoral practices of their elders.

Six, support women. Women have been politically marginalized in much of Africa, but when given the chance, have provided tremendous leadership in both civil society and the government. Studies have shown women politicians are significantly less corrupt than their male counterparts. NED is supporting several projects of IRI and NDI to cultivate women's political leadership in Africa, and can claim some tangible results. Also of note, with NED support the Solidarity Center working to expand the role of women within unions and labor associations in Africa. With NED funds, the Nigerian Federation of Women has produced a series of television videos (at a small fraction of what they would cost in the US) promoting women's participation in the elections. In Somaliland, women and youth organizations provide all the monitors for the successful elections that country has held. In Uganda, CEWIGO had impressive success in cultivating a new generation of female politicians.

Seven, don't pick a winner. We have often seen in Africa that today's democratic champion can readily become tomorrow's despot. Fred Chiluba of Zambia, Laurent Gbagbo of Cote d'Ivoire, Abdoulaye Wade of Senegal, Charles Taylor of Liberia, and most recently, Salva Kiir of South Sudan are notable examples. And even sympathetic, democratically elected leaders can fall prey to corruption, ineptitude, and scandal. NED respects pluralism and the political process in support of free and fair elections. Normally, party training is not conducted within 30 days of an election, funds may not support the candidacy of candidates for public office, and, by and large, whatever political loyalties our partners may have, their programs are non-partisan. Although NED opposes dictatorship, we do not advocate "regime change." Rather, we seek to support peaceful, democratic methods of political reform and development. A free and fair process is essential. More must be done to encourage good governance by democratically elected leaders.

Eight, the stakes in African elections can be very high. "The politics of the belly" still rules much of Africa, meaning that political office often affords the best opportunity for securing material wealth through patronage to clients and constituents. Losing an election can mean impoverishment, retribution, and worse. Hence, the enormous and sometimes violent efforts by some leaders and their followers to maintain power, and the perpetuation of corruption. For this reason, NED has supported many groups conducting investigative reporting, campaigning against corruption, and monitoring politicians' behavior. Other groups have stressed the notion of fair play, the opportunity for a second chance, and the fact that elections are not worth killing or dying for. Citizens also need to understand that elected officials are their servants and representatives, not their masters and patrons. They should not sell their vote for a bag of rice, as NAYMOTE, one of NED's long-time Liberian partners has successfully campaigned.

Nine, elections are not a panacea. Democratic elections do not necessarily bring about economic development, end corruption, or settle conflict, as has already been suggested. Democracy does not equal good governance. Democratically elected leaders may not adhere to democratic values, and they may not be great friends of the US. Conversely, undemocratic governments such as Ethiopia and Rwanda may provide good governance, reduce corruption, promote economic growth, and remain faithful US allies. Democracy may provide material benefits and stability over the long term, but we believe that it is democracy's intrinsic value, the freedom, dignity, and possibility for citizens to change leaders peacefully through elections that is most important, and that warrants strong American support. Thus NED has recently funded programs by NDI and IRI that are training Africa's political leaders in democratic values, as well as other leadership skills. NED's NGO partners frequently cite as their greatest impact the change in behavior and consciousness that they have brought about in their societies. Indeed, over the last 25 years, the democratic discourse in Africa has only grown more powerful. There are alternative "narratives" that are competing, such as the calls to end term limits and developmental authoritarianism, but elections continue to be the fundamental political reference.

Finally, Africans want elections. Elections matter. This is not to deny that in some countries election fatigue may have set in, that citizens are apprehensive about violence, or that corruption, impunity and a dearth of democratic dividends has not caused apathy. Many Africans may still vote along ethnic lines, or because the chief says to do so, out of loyalty to a political party, or without a full understanding of the democratic process. But anyone who has observed an African election can testify to the obvious commitment and enthusiasm of voters who may stand in line for hours in the hot sun to cast a ballot. Most of all, NED's partners support participation, citizen awareness, and mobilization. Considerable energy and money is invested in the process by governments and candidates, and the discussion in the media and the streets is often highly politicized, especially around election time, showing how important elections are considered to be. Afrobarometer polling shows that most Africans support democracy, even if they don't like their elected leaders. Elections may often be imperfect, democracy may still be a work in progress in Africa but NED and its grantees are optimistic about the future. Elections are and will continue to provide an important opportunity for change. In many countries on the continent where democracy has not yet consolidated, elections are an important driver for mobilizing participation, examining the record of accomplishment of government officials, and engaging the citizenry in taking responsibility for their own future.

Mr. Chairman, Ranking Member, and Members of the Committee, I look forward to your questions.

———

54

Mr. EMMER. Mr. Merloe.

STATEMENT OF MR. PATRICK MERLOE, DIRECTOR OF ELECTORAL PROGRAMS AND SENIOR ASSOCIATE, NATIONAL DEMOCRATIC INSTITUTE

Mr. MERLOE. Thank you, Mr. Chairman, Ranking Member Bass, distinguished members of the subcommittee and thank you for entering our full statements into the record. I associate myself with the comments of my colleagues and will not be repetitive of their remarks. Rather, I will concentrate on our concerns and eight recommendations that were presented in my statement.

Mr. Chairman, NDI has worked in 43 African countries on a wide variety of democracy-support programs including partnering with political parties, parliaments, civil society groups, and democratic reformers in government in more than 100 elections, plus we have observed international elections in Africa in 49 examples in 24 African countries.

The vast majority of these programs have been made possible by USAID, the NED, and DRL. And we greatly appreciate the trust that they have placed in the Institute to conduct programs that correspond with the vital interests of the people of this country and correspond with the democratic aspirations of the people of those African states.

I would like to use your example, Mr. Chairman, of Kenya, if I may. Kenya's 2007 elections demonstrated the horrific consequences of the lack of diligence by citizens and the international community. While the 2013 elections and the interim period between those two demonstrated the positive consequences of concerted efforts to build democratic institutions and processes.

If Kenya's 2017 elections are to move forward and avoid the possibility of falling back into violence and other problems, concerted efforts and focused international support is needed beginning now and moving forward. This is a lesson that should be applied across the continent when we look at elections and democratic support. The need for sustained, long-term, and multifaceted support for organizing peaceful, credible elections in Africa stands out in many examples beyond Kenya. The risks for failing to achieve them are extraordinarily high, while the benefits for governing, stability, and for inclusive authentic development are essential to progress on the continent.

Yet, there appears to be decreasing levels of support for democratic governance in Africa and a concentration on a small number of countries. This could have an unintended negative consequence, not just on organizing peaceful elections, but on democratic development, which is a cause for concern.

Public confidence and credibility of elections is vital to public trust in government. That trust is important for government stability which is essential to peace and security. This is particularly important today when we are challenged internationally by extraordinarily violent forces that reject democracy and human rights.

Support for democratic elections in Africa should build long-term democratic, political dynamics. The support should include encouraging reform of winner-take-all political systems and related politics. This can contribute to effective democracy that roots out corruption, improves lives, and reduces the possibility for political violence. Political parties that engage citizens on issues concerning improving their lives, rather than on personalities, on ethnicity, tribe, or religion are essential to developing peaceful, democratic elections and democratic governance in Africa. Electoral support needs to help political parties build capacities, structures, and communication mechanisms in this respect.

Party programming needs to encompass political steps that lead to the camps eschewing electoral violence. Support also should bolster parties' capacity to improve legal frameworks to verify the accuracy of key electoral processes and to gather the evidence that is necessary to pursue effective legal redress.

Mr. Chairman, citizen election monitoring is critical to support for African elections. Monitoring and advocacy by African citizen groups are making a sustained contribution to peaceful, credible elections by witnessing key election processes over the long arc of elections, for analyzing electoral data, making and reporting findings, and for making recommendations for improvements in electoral and political processes. Election monitoring spread across the continent through a peer-to-peer approach that included assistance to developing expertise and then helping experts move to other countries to bring with them the best techniques and core organizational structures that are needed. NDI's experience in assisting those groups demonstrates that organizational development and skills consolidation is difficult to sustain when support is limited to short periods immediately before elections.

Many of these groups have formed subregional networks. Those networks help each other and they all come together in the Global Network for Citizen Election Monitoring (GNDEM), which has over 200 member organizations in 82 countries, 37 of them in Africa. In that network, they provide skill sharing, best practices, they adopt innovations, and they build solidarity for one another when pressure comes upon those groups.

Electoral support should focus on aiding these groups and on the professional development of these regional and global networks based upon the ethical foundations that are provided in the Declaration of Global Principles that GNDEM, the global network, has provided, launched by the United Nations Secretariat in 2012.

Mr. Chairman, parallel vote tabulations, as Mr. Postel mentioned, by citizen organizations play a key role in decreasing political volatility and mitigating potential for violence. The precision of PVTs in gauging whether the voting and counting processes support an honest result and in projecting statistically with large degrees of confidence and low margins of error, are important for building public confidence in elections as was the case cited most recently in Zambia, but also it has been true in Ghana and other places around the continent. In fact, NDI has assisted the successful implementation of 38 parallel vote tabulations in more than 11 African countries, and these techniques are being taken up in other places. Support for Africa elections should prioritize the assistance to these nonpartisan election monitoring groups, particularly to take up systematic assessments of election processes.

Let me conclude by addressing briefly international election observation, which can play an important role in achieving peaceful, credible elections in Africa. The key organizations that engage in international observation come together in coordinating their efforts increasingly and harmonizing their findings in a process that is built around the Declaration of Principles for International Election Observations launched at the United Nations Secretariat in 2005. The African Union, ECOWAS, Francophonie, and other African groups come together in this process with EU, the OSCE, the OAS, Carter Center, NDI, and the other convening organizations in order to help build best practices and some peer accountability. Support for African elections should provide assistance for key organizations to fully engage in that implementation process. This could significantly reduce the potential for well-known international organizations issuing different findings about African elections. Thank you, Mr. Chairman.

[The prepared statement of Mr. Merloe follows:]

Statement of Patrick Merloe

Senior Associate and Director of Electoral Programs

NATIONAL DEMOCRATIC INSTITUTE (NDI)

before the

UNITED STATES HOUSE OF REPRESENTATIVES
COMMITTEE ON FOREIGN AFFAIRS
SUBCOMMITTEE ON AFRICA, GLOBAL HEALTH, GLOBAL HUMAN RIGHTS,
AND INTERNATIONAL ORGANIZATIONS

March 18, 2015

U.S. ELECTION SUPPORT IN AFRICA

Mr. Chairman, Members of the Subcommittee, thank you for this opportunity to address the important topic of U.S. election support in Africa. The National Democratic Institute (NDI) has worked in 43 African countries since the late 1980s on a wide variety of programs to help strengthen democratic development, including achieving peaceful, credible elections. NDI has partnered with political parties, parliaments, civil society groups and democratic reformers in government in more than 100 African elections, and with the March 28 polls in Nigeria NDI will have engaged in international observation activities for 49 elections in 24 African nations. Presently the Institute is conducting programs in 20 African states, plus several regional programs. Many of these ongoing programs include an electoral focus.

The vast majority of these NDI programs were made possible by the support of the United States government through the United States Agency for International Development (USAID), the National Endowment for Democracy (NED) and the Department of State's Bureau of Democracy, Human Rights and Labor (DRL). NDI greatly appreciates the trust that those agencies have placed in the Institute to conduct programs that are consistent with the vital interests of the people of this country and that advance democratic aspirations of the people in those African nations – including for peaceful, credible elections. We also greatly appreciate the leadership that this Subcommittee provides and thank you for convening today's hearing.

More than 25 elections are scheduled in African countries in the 21 months between now and the end of 2016. Nigeria's polls are set for just 10 days from this hearing. Other countries also face volatile political environments, like the Central African Republic, or are on a sensitive path, recovering from widespread violence, like Cote d'Ivoire. Some countries face electoral credibility challenges posed by little or closing political space, like Ethiopia. Still others, such as Benin and Ghana, where elections are scheduled for next year, are developing a history of credible elections. While the contexts differ for elections across the Continent, all of them are sensitive and merit attention. Kenya's 2007 elections demonstrated the horrific consequences of a lack of vigilance by citizens and the international community, while its 2013 elections demonstrated the positive consequences of concerted efforts to build democratic institutions and processes, along with a rejection of violence. If Kenya's 2017 elections are to demonstrate further progress, and avoid the risk of falling backward, continued robust engagement by citizens with focused international support will be required. This is a lesson that should be applied in electoral support across the Continent.

The need for sustained, long-term and multifaceted support for organizing peaceful, credible elections in Africa stands out in many examples beyond Kenya. The risks for failing to achieve them are extraordinarily high, while the benefits for governmental stability and inclusive, authentic development are essential to progress on the Continent. Yet, there appears to be a decrease in levels of support for democratic governance in Africa and a concentration on a small number of countries. This could have an unintended effect on holding peaceful, credible elections, which is a cause for concern.

Public confidence in the credibility of elections is vital to public trust in government. That trust is important for governmental stability, which elections should help secure. Governments in Africa, as elsewhere, are obliged by their constitutions and international obligations to hold genuine elections, which is a right of the people. The international community has keen interests in governmental stability, which relates to peace and security, and it has interests in promoting fundamental rights. This is particularly important today, when international security is facing critical challenges from extraordinarily violent forces that reject democracy and human rights.

NDI's work in Africa, as elsewhere, often engages in consensus building to allow elections to preform two essential roles: (1) to provide the vehicle through which the people express their will as to who is to have the authority to govern; and (2) to resolve peacefully the competition for control of governmental powers. NDI works with African partners on other aspects of elections that reinforce these roles, including: (a) helping to ensure that the population can make free and informed political choices based on issues that are central to improving peoples' lives; and (b) enhancing citizen participation in electoral processes to safeguard electoral integrity and build public trust in elections and the governments that result from them.

Support for democratic elections in Africa should build longer-term democratic political dynamics that result in responsive, accountable governance. A wide variety of processes and institutions must be engaged over a relatively long period of time to organize peaceful, credible elections, and a range of rights and responsibilities of citizenship must be exercised for elections to be genuine. In effect, the processes surrounding elections reflect how those in government and those competing for that power relate to each other and, more importantly, how they respect the citizenry. Support for peaceful, credible elections must take this into account, not separate elections from the broader political dynamic in a country and should seek to build capacities and processes that reach beyond elections in a narrow sense.

An important element of support for peaceful, credible elections in Africa should be to encourage reform of winner-take-all governance structures and electoral systems. Divisions of powers among branches of government, including checks and balances and decentralizing governmental powers, as well as systems that provide significant roles for traditionally marginalized populations, are important for achieving peaceful, credible elections. This can contribute to effective democracy that roots out corruption, improves lives and is genuinely representative.

The integrity of elections depends on diverse processes. They include, for example, those individualized procedures needed to document a person's birth and residence, which are required to establish candidacy or rightful place on a voter registry, as well as data intensive processes needed to verify the accuracy of the voter registry, the fairness of ballot access, whether electoral districts ensure equality of the vote and whether the results were tabulated accurately.

Electoral integrity depends on the freedom of political expression and the ability to organize campaigns, as well as the political impartiality of government controlled media, the use of state resources and other issues of political finance, in addition to the impartiality and competence of those administering the country's elections.

The effective and impartial functioning of law enforcement agencies and security forces are critical to whether political contestants can freely compete and citizens can vote free of fear of violence or political retribution. Electoral integrity also depends on whether courts and administrative complaint mechanisms deliver timely and otherwise effective redress for infringements of election related rights and accountability for electoral abuses. This illustrates how equality before the law and equal protection of the law are related to holding genuine elections. Unless competitors feel they have a fair chance to win and to redress electoral grievances, they may turn to violent means to gain power.

Removing barriers to participation of marginalized populations and all citizens regardless of their political preferences is at the core of genuine elections. This highlights the importance of gender equality in electoral support as well as examining each country's political culture to identify other populations and attitudes towards youth participation. Enfranchisement requires inclusion without discrimination or unreasonable restriction. Inclusiveness is the essence of universal and equal suffrage and is a critical challenge in African countries as it as around the world.

While no election is perfect, positive developments across these processes move a country toward peaceful, credible elections and stable democratic governance. Just as robust support is needed to help ensure impartial and effective administration of all the complex, relatively costly and time sensitive elements of electoral management – for elections to be peaceful and credible in Africa and elsewhere, support is essential to build this broader democratic political dynamic.

Political parties that understand the pressing needs of the population and that engage with citizens on issues that concern improving living conditions – rather than conducting politics based on personalities, ethnicity, tribe or religion – are essential to developing peaceful, credible elections and democratic governance in Africa. Electoral support needs to help parties develop capacities, structures and communication mechanisms in this respect. This requires programs that begin years before and stretch well beyond elections.

Political party programming also needs to encompass dialogue among the competing camps to eschew engaging in violence, to train party activists to reject violence and to discipline supporters who violate the admonition. Facilitating public anti-violence agreements among parties and candidates should be part of that support, which should also help ensure that codes of electoral conduct are enforced by election authorities, prosecutors and the courts. Such rule of law support in the electoral context can promote accountability more broadly and enhance public confidence in African elections. Inter-party liaison committees with election authorities, party youth academies and inter-party women's leadership and youth alliances can contribute significantly to anti-violence efforts.

Political party support also should bolster parties' roles in ensuring electoral integrity. Parties' capacities to analyze and advocate for improvements in legal frameworks for elections, to analyze the fairness of electoral boundaries, to verify the accuracy of the voter registry and to gather in a timely manner required evidence of electoral violations and pursue effective legal redress also are needed elements of electoral support. Election-day activities of party and candidate poll watchers also need to meet the evidence-based and timely requirements of verifying polling procedures and the accuracy of official voting results.

Electoral support in Africa needs to adopt longer term work with political parties and needs to break down silos between developing issue-oriented ties with the population, violence prevention and defending electoral integrity through rule of law approaches.

Citizen election monitoring is a crucial aspect of support for African elections. People have a right to genuine elections, and they have a right to <u>know</u> that elections are genuine. Otherwise, the population must rely on blind faith or rumors – rather than public knowledge – in deciding whether to trust electoral results or whether to heed the calls of those who reject them. Across the Continent – where there is not a history of credible elections and public confidence is not well established in governmental institutions or political parties – civil society organizations are stepping forward to monitor electoral processes, present analysis about their quality and offer recommendations for improving elections. Monitoring and advocacy by these groups are making sustained contributions to developing governmental and political accountability in and beyond elections.

Election monitoring by citizen groups has occurred in at least 32 African countries. NDI facilitated the spread of citizen election monitoring on the Continent, using a peer-to-peer approach. That included aiding groups in developing expertise and bringing experts from one country to help groups in other places to adopt election monitoring techniques and core organizational capacities. The Institute also encouraged these groups to form the West Africa Election Observer Network (WAEON) with members groups in 11 countries, SADC Election Support Network (SADC-ESN) with member groups in 14 countries and the East and Horn of Africa Elections Observers Network (E-HORN) with member groups in four countries. Groups in North Africa work in networks with Middle Eastern organizations, and all are united in the Global Network of Domestic Election Monitors (GNDEM), which has over 200 member organizations from 82 countries, plus their various regional networks. GNDEM members have mobilized well over 3 million citizen election observers, including hundreds of thousands across Africa.

These networks provide mechanisms for sharing best practices within Africa's sub-regions and across the Continent, to adopt innovations from other parts of the world while offering knowledge gained in African experiences and building solidarity for this type of specialized human rights defense. Support from USAID has been instrumental for citizen election monitoring efforts in specific countries, while the NED has provided support for developing regional networks and GNDEM, and DRL provided a recent grant that allowed GNDEM and NDI to bring together key activists from Africa's three sub-regional networks for skills building on: verifying the quality of election-day processes and accuracy of official results through use of representative statistical samples ("parallel vote tabulations" or PVTs); monitoring biometric voter registration; and advocating for timely citizen access to key electoral data (an open government/open electoral data initiative).

PVTs by nonpartisan citizen election monitors play a key role in decreasing political volatility about election results and building public confidence in election-day processes, thus mitigating potentials for violence. NDI has assisted the successful implementation of 38 PVTs in 11 African countries, including Zambia's recent presidential election and prior elections, Malawi's recent elections and prior elections, Kenya's 2013 elections and 2010 constitutional referendum as well as elections in Ghana, Sierra Leone, Senegal and Uganda. A PVT was conducted for Nigeria's 2011 elections, and one is being organized for the upcoming presidential election. The PVT for Zimbabwe's 2008 first round election played the extraordinary role of demonstrating that President Mugabe came in second and that a run-off was required.

The precision of PVTs in (a) assessing the quality of election-day voting processes (gauging whether they support an honest result) and (b) projecting with narrow margins of error and high degrees of confidence what accurate official results should be, provides a crucial contribution to achieving peaceful, credible elections in Africa and elsewhere. The use of rapid information communications technologies (ICTs), including social media, in informing the public of findings also contributes to public knowledge and confidence in African elections. Plus, like other aspects of citizen election monitoring, PVTs provide an organizational structure, critical skills and credibility for citizen groups to conduct other types of evidence-based governmental accountability functions.

Like other areas of electoral support, work with citizen election monitors, including building skills and networks for systematic techniques, requires longer term engagement and sharing the experiences of emerging experts with activists in other countries. NDI's experience on the Continent demonstrates that organizational development and skills consolidation is difficult to sustain when support is limited to short periods immediately preceding an election.

Support for African elections should prioritize assistance to nonpartisan citizen election monitoring, particularly efforts that employ systematic assessment methods (such as PVTs and voter register verifications), and that engage in political violence monitoring and mitigation, political finance monitoring and other activities that address the integrity of key electoral processes. Support should also focus on aiding the professional development of sub-regional networks of citizen election monitors and other civil society organizations that dedicate themselves to peaceful, credible elections. GNDEM developed the *Declaration of Global Principles for Nonpartisan Election Observation and Monitoring by Citizen Organizations* to provide the ethical basis and methodological guide for credible citizen election monitoring, and African citizen election monitoring organizations and their networks should be supported in the implementation process and capacity building efforts around the declaration.

Open government and open government data, including open electoral data, are central to fighting corruption and achieving peaceful, credible elections. United States support for African elections should assist efforts at furthering these principles of electoral transparency. If political party agents, citizen election monitors and the media are not allowed to witness the various election processes and are not provided timely and effective access to electoral data, it is impossible to determine whether elections are trustworthy. The Electoral Commission of South Africa (the IEC) and other electoral related governmental bodies are global leaders on these subjects, and other positive examples exist on the Continent. International support should provide incentives for African election commissions (election management bodies, EMBs), citizen election monitors, political parties and other stakeholders to advance these principles in practical ways.

International election observation can play an important role in achieving peaceful, credible elections in Africa. The leading intergovernmental and international nongovernmental organizations that conduct election observation are increasingly coordinating their efforts and harmonizing their findings. These developments are the result of an ongoing implementation process built around *the Declaration of Principles for International Election Observation,* launched at the UN Secretariat in 2005, now endorsed by 49 organizations and recognized with appreciation in three UN General Assembly (UNGA) resolutions for its contributions to improving the field. The United States led the efforts around those UNGA resolutions.

The African Union, ECOWAS and the International Organization of La Francophonie (OIF) endorse the Declaration, which brings them into contact with the implementation process convening members, including among others the EU, OSCE's Office for

Democratic Institutions and Human Rights (ODIHR), UN Electoral Assistance Division, Carter Center and NDI. Each organization pays its way for participating in the process. International support for African elections should provide assistance for key organizations to engage fully in the process as well as to urge African organizations to implement the methodologies provided in the declaration. This could significantly increase their capacities and reduce the potential of well-known international election observation organizations from issuing differing findings about specific African elections.

———————

Mr. EMMER. Thank you, Mr. Merloe.

I will recognize myself to start. I will note that Mr. Clawson has joined the subcommittee and everybody this morning had many different conflicts.

Mr. CLAWSON. I had three at once, so please don't take offense. Sorry about that.

Mr. EMMER. If you have any opening remarks that you want to make at this point?

Mr. CLAWSON. I never come to a party late and then start talking right away. I will jump in the game in a little while. I am glad you all came and glad for the service that you all do for so many folks around the world, so thank you for coming today. Thanks.

Mr. EMMER. Mr. Sweeney, I want to start with you. You made the reference that young Africans' expectations are higher. I think I know what that means, but could you just expand on that part of your testimony?

Mr. SWEENEY. Thank you, Mr. Chairman. Simply put, the patience of the younger generation around the world is much lower than the patience of old folks like myself. Particularly in Africa, we are seeing an expectation, a demand, that things change and things change quickly. And that means that the political process has to be responsive to those demands or else they drop out. And given the size of that population, that then becomes a threat to the stability of their countries and their cultures going forward because they will come back into the system in some way, in an angry way, perhaps, as we have seen in other countries.

In Africa, when you look at the demographics, and particularly go back to South Africa where in talking with friends of mine on the South African Election Commission, I said what is your greatest challenge? And they said a majority of voters have no memory of apartheid. They have no memory of Nelson Mandela's entire struggle because they came of age since he was elected President. That is an enormous challenge in terms of civic education, in terms of trying to do outreach among those citizens. In other countries in the Middle East, we see the same problem right now where people have participated in elections, those elections have not had consequences that they imagined or desire, and they are dropping out of the process.

Mr. EMMER. And I appreciate you focusing it on Africa and some other places, but when you opened it, I think the ranking member and I agree that I think the statement is applicable all around the globe that the younger folks have less patience.

Ms. BASS. We were young once. We remember that.

Mr. EMMER. I am still very young, but thank you for recognizing that.

Mr. Sweeney, USAID has a booklet acknowledging the entirety of the election cycle, so the understanding and importance of the whole process. Do you believe funding is the major reason why such programming is more limited than it might be?

Mr. SWEENEY. I think there is a combination, sir. The first, obviously, is funding. All development agencies around the world engage in democracy and governance have had funding issues over the course of the last few years, both because of the fiscal crisis and competing demands.

The second is, candidly, this field has become much more robust and we have become much more sophisticated and as such all of the organizations have spawned other organizations so there is a greater demand than there was say when I was doing my first mission with NDI and IRI doing political training in Hungary and the Berlin Wall was still up. This investment in the philosophy of democracy has attracted hundreds of organizations, both global and national, that are doing great work. And that places greater demands on grant-making organizations be they NED or USAID or any of the other foundations or international donors.

Mr. EMMER. Thank you. Ms. Birkle, you state that parties are too personality driven. By the way, Mr. Merloe referenced this as well. And we will stay on this, but it caught me, the quote caught me that we need people to focus on campaign issues, rather than personalities. I think that is probably a global issue, too.

Ms. BASS. Sounds familiar.

Mr. EMMER. Yes, just a little bit. But if you can, has there been measurable success in helping African political parties create coherent party platforms that build sustainable party structures to select viable candidates?

Ms. BIRKLE. Thank you. There has been success. I would even point to limited success currently in Nigeria where we have been working with USAID funding over the past 2 or 3 years and even when our programs first started in the late '90s with political parties in Nigeria, to really have them embrace internal party reforms and the notion of issue based political parties. We have been able to have public opinion polls in several countries that have helped political parties understand the importance of issues and what that means to electorates and how they can devise campaigns around the issues to help them run more effective campaigns and really to encourage greater participation from the electorate.

We just finished a public opinion survey in Uganda that will be released later this week. We hope that that is going to serve as a basis for many of the Ugandan political parties as they look to elections next year.

Mr. EMMER. Mr. Merloe, since you brought up this as well, do you have anything you want to add?

Mr. MERLOE. I think it is incredibly important that we look at political parties over the arc of time. Most of the countries that we are talking about in Africa started with relatively low levels of political organization. Of course, South Africa was different. The liberation movements were very well organized and needed to make the transition to seeking votes at the ballot box which IRI and NDI and others helped to do. But that level of organization has not been present in many countries. So first we start with those people who are seeking governmental powers which are sometimes coming out of those conflicts, where we are looking at an armed basis for competing for powers. And with that, there needs to be a kind of transition work that brings into the process lots of the population to mitigate the potentials for violence, including civil society playing a critical role. You can get through the transition elections and help those political organizations begin to take on qualities that are more like political parties.

In other places, where you are starting with personality-driven politics, which as you noted is very well established around the world, it is helping people see that if they each stand separately, they are likely to divide the population that might support the change in their country, so learning how to come together in coalitions becomes a very important activity. And then, of course, if a coalition succeeds as happened in Kenya three elections ago, you have to help them learn how to be a governing coalition, which is a very complicated process in Parliament. So all of these things are necessary, and we have to work very hard on it. Just last week in South Africa, we brought together the secretary generals of political parties, opposing and government political parties, from 14 countries in the SADC region in order to try to determine what is an agenda for strengthening parties looking forward on the continent in the next 10 years. This is a constant process.

Mr. EMMER. Mr. Robinson, I have got one for you. You state in various ways that elections are not the be all end all of democracy. I think you started your testimony with that. In what way does any defunding complement USAID funding to ensure that democratic processes in Africa are built from the grassroots up and not just from the top down, kind of continuing on like Mr. Merloe just was?

Mr. ROBINSON. Thank you for your question, Mr. Chairman. I think it is recognizing that it is a long term, incremental process when you start talking about ideas and concepts and seating them. So what we do is we look at grassroots organizations to begin that process in areas and places where people haven't been exposed to these ideas. And by slowly tilling that soil, by pushing these concepts out there, at the request of people who submit proposals, it should be repeated that the endowment does not tell people what to do. We receive proposals from people, the programs that they want to implement. And so what we do is we till that soil, the concepts go out there, and then when some of our partner organizations come in and they have a very focused strategy on elections, on processes, the ground is ready. People are ready to engage with the actors that are in governing positions.

Mr. EMMER. Thank you. At this point, I will recognize the ranking member for 5 minutes.

Ms. BASS. Thank you. I just have a few questions that are kind of all over the place. I was thinking of the Nigeria election coming up. How confident are you, and I would throw that open to anybody who would like to answer, about the security issue. We understand that was the reason the elections were postponed, so what has happened?

Mr. SWEENEY. I will take a first stab. The security situation, if you really follow the press and reports from the military, they are confident, at least so far that they have been successful over the course of the last 6 weeks. Of course, we are dealing with a terrorist organization that has threatened to engage in disruption of the election process and as we all know, terrorists only need one incident in order to claim some success.

Nigeria also has a history of election violence between parties and factions. I suspect we will see some of that as well, so discerning what was normal crime on election day that does happen everywhere around the world versus electoral-related violence versus terrorist activities will be subject of some inquiry.

There are numerous efforts, including some by IFES, to try and chronicle this to be able to exchange information very, very quickly using social media and other forums. The INEC itself has a command center in partnership with the security forces, so I think the entire country will be on alert as best it can be.

Ms. BASS. Is anybody aware of what is happening in Sierra Leone? The Vice President, I guess, was just dismissed. He was seeking asylum at the U.S. Embassy. I didn't know if any of you were aware of that which I think is unfortunate.

Burkina Faso, do you think that what happened there will have a chilling effect or will it be hopeful? In other words, in countries that might be considering delaying their elections, given what happened there, do you think that sends a signal that maybe that is not the best idea or does it send the other message which is a chilling effect to the population to just, you know, go along and cooperate?

Mr. Robinson?

Mr. ROBINSON. I think you have seen the impact of what happened in Burkina Faso and DRC with the arrest that took place the other day. Some of the people that were engaged in Burkina Faso were there at the event and I think there is the perception by countries that are considering delaying elections, even in a round about way as they were in DRC that they view this as a threat. And so yes, this has been—they are taking notice, authoritarian leaders, in particular, across the continent.

Ms. BASS. How do you think the populations are responding?

Mr. ROBINSON. The populations, as was said earlier, people are responding like hey, it is happening elsewhere. This is exciting. But in Africa when someone comes down on you hard, they come down on you hard and they shoot live ammunition into crowds or people are just simply disappeared. So they take that to heart because they have experienced it time and time again.

Ms. BASS. Mr. Merloe or Ms. Birkle?

Mr. MERLOE. Thank you, ranking member. I believe that Eric summarized it very, very well. On the one hand there is a tug of war between people who would impose authoritarian regimes and people who have over the arc of history struggled to have governments that are representative of the population. And what happened in Burkina Faso, with people coming to the street, I think in many ways, inspired people not just in Africa, but also those who learned of it around the world. And as my colleague sitting over here, Dr. Keith Jennings, likes to say, "I haven't seen many examples of people coming to the streets demanding more authoritarianism."

So they are not always successful. Sometimes, as we have seen in Egypt, they are beaten back. Sometimes they are attacked, as we have seen in other countries like in Ukraine being attacked. But nonetheless, what we see around the world is a consistent drive for having representative government.

Now, we have a little bit of a discussion that is going on around this town about democratic recession, that in the last 9 years we haven't seen as many dramatic breakthroughs as we have in the

10 or 20 years before that. But if we look at this over the time
when World War II ended, when there were less than a dozen democracies after fighting the horrendous authoritarianism in the
Second War World, the Berlin Wall was going up then, and military dictatorships were being established around the world. Colonialism was trying to come back and from that arc until today
there have been tremendous progress. And I think that is very true
on the African continent. My work goes around the world, but in
23 African countries, I find this to be more inspiring than I see
troubling.

Ms. BASS. A couple more, and this is directed to you. You were
asking—you were talking about the Nigerian parties and identi-
fying issues and the Ugandan political parties and I just wanted
to know if you could expand on that and one place I would like to
go, I have never quite understood, I know NDI and IRI sometimes
work in the same countries, but I really don't know what you do
differently. And when you were talking about political positions
and all that it certainly piqued my curiosity, so what are you guys
doing?

Ms. BIRKLE. Thank you. In terms of IRI and NDI, we work very
closely in many, many countries and Nigeria is a good example of
that. Uganda, Kenya, there is a whole host of countries where we
are together, but there are some countries where we are not. And
some of that has just been choices because of restricted funding
amounts or divisions of leadership to engage in one country or not
another. And that is different globally. But in general, and with the
International Foundation for Electoral Systems and also with our
NED partners, there is a real very healthy sense of camaraderie
and competition amongst the institutes in the countries where we
work.

Ms. BASS. So what perspectives do you bring? I mean I think you
know where I am going. Do you bring political positions? Because
when you talked about that, that is what I was wondering.

Ms. BIRKLE. We don't. You know, once we are working overseas,
we really are working around issues that are germane to those
countries. And so when I am conducting and IRI is conducting political party survey research, for example, it is really based on the
issues that the people of those countries are telling us are important to them.

Ms. BASS. I would love to see those surveys.

Ms. BIRKLE. Certainly.

Ms. BASS. And I don't mean to just—I referenced you because
you mentioned that, but you might do issues that are germane to
the countries, but how you interpret those issues, so I would direct
that to you, Mr. Merloe, where you come from and how you interpret that.

Mr. MERLOE. Good question. NDI has worked since our founding
in what you might say is a multi-ideological fashion. We are associ-
ated with the political party internationals across the spectrum and
often bring them together in our work. We integrate Republicans
and Democrats and people from various political parties around the
world into our work. And when we are working with political parties on how to take an issue orientation toward their citizens, what
we try to help them to do is face outward to the citizens and get

citizen input. Let the citizens define what are the critical issues for them, and then help those parties look at research, this side and that, and formulate their own positions. What we don't do is: IRI does not work with parties on the right, and NDI work with parties on the left. We work across the political spectrum to promote democratic, political dynamics.

Ms. BASS. So you are going to come here and help us?

Mr. MERLOE. We are not allowed to work inside the United States.

Ms. BASS. Okay, thank you very much. I appreciate it. I yield back.

Mr. EMMER. Thank you, ranking member. The Chair recognizes Representative Clawson for 5 minutes.

Mr. CLAWSON. So if I missed something that you all said in your openings, if I am repetitive in some way, you all will forgive me because I wasn't here, okay? So as I think about what I have read about what you all do, how you get it accomplished, I draw from my own experience in the private sector for many years and my own experience in my many visits to Africa.

Kind of my starting point is socialism destroys wealth and it is tough to bring people up that way. Private enterprise, if it is crony capitalism is unfair and it causes a lot of people consternation because they don't have private property rights and people that want to get ahead don't really have a shot because those in power have got all the economic resources for themselves. And that too often, we are in one place or another. We are way too socialistic which destroys wealth because it ignores competitive marketplaces. Or we are in the crony capitalism bucket where bunches of a small amount of people have got it all for themselves and then everybody else is in the middle suffering.

And then I say to myself well, try to do elections in that environment. Can you really do that? And if I was sitting in you all's chair I would say in the countries where you don't have private property rights, economic opportunity for folks, what is the point of trying to get elections, you know? People just are going to get stamped down anyway.

And so it kind of feels like you have to narrow where you want to shoot and use your resources to where there is a match of economic opportunity with electoral opportunity. I am not even sure that is a word. Am I making sense to you all? And if I am, what does that mean in your own efforts and why are you laughing at me right now? If my question is way off base, you tell me, but it is how I think about things. Go ahead.

Mr. ROBINSON. Thank you for your question. I guess I will start by saying that one of the things you are addressing is for NED and people with whom we work on the continent, it is the issue of corruption and I think looking at the issue of crony capitalism it is paralyzing. What happens when you have so much money flowing to only a few people and the business sector is not on a level playing field. People can't compete with their own ideas.

Mr. CLAWSON. And just to interrupt, the typical poor voter equates democracy with that crony capitalism?

Mr. ROBINSON. What they see is wow, this dream of democracy that we have had for decades, is this what it is? And that is exactly it. This democratic dispensation isn't coming through. However, a lot of them, just like many people around the world are able to distinguish they don't say oh, you are an American, I don't like you. They are able to separate things out. And people are also able to say hey, we still want the vote.

Someone referred to Afrobarometer statistics. Afrobarometer shows very clearly that Africans support democracy. Africans support the right to vote. And what we are looking at right now is how do we do more forensic accounting in terms of the money that we give in Africa? How do we get them to engage to be more transparent in terms of how money goes in and how their relationships are conducted so that money is spent in the country to build institutions, to build confidence and trust in the institutions? And when you have again, like you said, crony capitalism or people controlling all aspects of the state, it is very difficult to make it happen.

Mr. CLAWSON. Is my correlation correct or am I all wet? Is there a higher to what you just said? Is there a higher degree of involvement or desire to be involved in the political process when there is economic opportunity for everyone? Or is it more when there is less because people want change and they are more desperate or do you know? Yes, sir.

Mr. SWEENEY. First of all, Congressman, I never call a Congressman who is asking a question all wet.

Mr. CLAWSON. But you are about to.

Mr. SWEENEY. No, I am not, sir. But I am going to say that we are all—all of us, without choosing—all of us are in the political change business. All of us are in the optimism business that you can build a democratic process where all citizens have the opportunity to exercise their political right and their human right to choose the leaders of their society. And that change usually comes about in reaction to the two extremes that you described the crony capitalism where the wealth of the country is held by only a few and not shared with the general society.

Mr. CLAWSON. And I am a Republican and that is wrong.

Just for the record.

Mr. SWEENEY. I understand that, sir. I completely understand that. And I think your own interest in this topic as evidenced by you being here is a statement about your attitudes toward these two extremes, the one being where the country is being—the wealth and the power is being held by a few to the exclusion of the demands and ambitions of everyone else, or the wealth and the power is so distributed in such a way that no one has any opportunity and ambitions are frustrated. That then results in a consensus for change and all of us have been involved in some ways who deal with political parties or with civil societies or with public institutions and then making that process of change peaceful and legitimate and accountable and transparent and free and fair and that is a challenge of civil society. That is a challenge for political parties. That is a challenge to the news media. That is a challenge to the judiciary. And in my case, that is a challenge to the public servants who are trying to stage the election and make sure that everyone's vote is cast and counted in a completely transparent and professional fashion to the satisfaction of all other elements.

71

Mr. CLAWSON [presiding]. Can I finish in your absence? If you need to go, go. You all don't mind staying another minute? Half the room is going to leave right now, but go ahead, continue. What you are saying is, well, go ahead, either of the other two that haven't spoken have anything to add to that?

Ms. BIRKLE. Well, I would just add and thank you for the thoughtful question. We recognize very much that there are limited resources that we have to do our work overseas. And each of our organizations needs to be very strategic about where we choose to work because there are limited resources. And then also to point out that we really do view nations as a process. And they are only one very important stage of the democratic development process. And while we are talking about elections today, there is a whole host of work that we will do throughout the course of an election cycle to encourage citizen engagement and citizen questioning of their elected officials, and programs that encourage citizens to hold their elected officials accountable and to engage during campaigns and closer to elections through debates, for example, or other outreach programs. So citizens start to really understand the issues matter to them and that their vote is going to matter ultimately on how they are governed and how that will impact their life.

Mr. MERLOE. As I was reflecting, sir, on your question and I have had the honor of sitting with former President George W. Bush as he was setting up the Bush Institute. And I have had the honor of sitting with President Carter and talking about these kinds of things. It is not a question of what political point of view you have from this country. I think you are right. There is an interrelationship on many of these points.

What really we are talking about is human dignity and people want human dignity. They want some control over what happens to their lives. They don't want to be exploited one way or the other, whether it is a one-party state or whether it is a military dictatorship.

And in a sense, I agree with my colleagues that have been in the private sector, though I have been in this work for some years. You have to be strategic. You want your energies to create something that is valuable so that you feel that it has been a good use of your time and efforts.

There are countries where there are minimal things that we can do. There are nonetheless people in those countries who want dignity and want some kind of a representative government rather than what they have got. And there are some ways of working with them, remotely in small ways and so on. In other places, you can see that there is an opportunity to help those people take that next step. And when they ask you to do that, it is an honor to be able to help them out in the process. I am trying to get at the essence of what I thought was your question. It is a marathon.

Yesterday, we met at NDI, and I am sure my colleagues and some people on the Hill met with, Mr. Morgan Tsvangirai, a former Prime Minister of Zimbabwe who has been trying to get into government there. And part of what he said is this is a marathon: "We may be coming to the last 5 miles. That is when you need support the most." And so there really is a challenge, country by country as to what you might be able to do that is helpful.

Mr. CLAWSON. Even after hearing you speak, I think governance, freedom, and economic growth are all tied together. There are great models of economic growth that ignore human rights, human dignity, and have governance by a small amount of people. And as I watch Africa develop, I am always worried that that model could be adopted if the correct crony capitalistic model that puts all the wealth in very little hands and the governance as well causes folks or causes the military or some other entity. And so anything I can do to help, I mean I am just a Congressman, right? But anything I can do to help I am all for what you are doing. I think it is a big deal.

I hope that, if anything, my few comments today help you think about how to be selective about which countries and where the ground is most fertile to spend these kind of dollars in your own effort.

And the other thing I guess I would say is the people out there doing this on the ground, that is not easy work, right, under very difficult circumstances. And so, if you will pass along my compliments in that regard, these are folks that have foregone creature comforts and other things to do difficult things in difficult environments. It is always easy in DC for us to forget that, right? It is easy to criticize those that are working hard for the benefit of their fellow men and women. So if you will pass that along for me, I am done with my little comments today and appreciate everything you all are doing. And I will gavel it out, right? The subcommittee is adjourned, right? This is the first I have ever got to do this, you all.

[Whereupon, at 12:06 p.m., the subcommittee adjourned.]

APPENDIX

MATERIAL SUBMITTED FOR THE RECORD

SUBCOMMITTEE HEARING NOTICE
COMMITTEE ON FOREIGN AFFAIRS
U.S. HOUSE OF REPRESENTATIVES
WASHINGTON, DC 20515-6128

Subcommittee on Africa, Global Health, Global Human Rights, and International Organizations
Christopher H. Smith (R-NJ), Chairman

March 18, 2015

TO: MEMBERS OF THE COMMITTEE ON FOREIGN AFFAIRS

You are respectfully requested to attend an OPEN hearing of the Committee on Foreign Affairs, to be held by the Subcommittee on Africa, Global Health, Global Human Rights, and International Organizations in Room 2255 of the Rayburn House Office Building (and available live on the Committee website at http://www.ForeignAffairs.house.gov):

DATE: Wednesday, March 18, 2015

TIME: 10:15 a.m.

SUBJECT: U.S. Election Support in Africa

WITNESSES: Panel I
The Honorable Eric G. Postel
Assistant to the Administrator
Bureau for Africa
U.S. Agency for International Development

Panel II
Mr. William Sweeney
President and Chief Executive Officer
International Foundation for Electoral Systems

Ms. Gretchen Birkle
Regional Director for Africa
International Republican Institute

Mr. Eric Robinson
Senior Program Officer for East and Horn of Africa
National Endowment for Democracy

Mr. Patrick Merloe
Director of Electoral Programs and Senior Associate
National Democratic Institute

By Direction of the Chairman

The Committee on Foreign Affairs seeks to make its facilities accessible to persons with disabilities. If you are in need of special accommodations, please call 202/225-5021 at least four business days in advance of the event, whenever practicable. Questions with regard to special accommodations in general (including availability of Committee materials in alternative formats and assistive listening devices) may be directed to the Committee.

COMMITTEE ON FOREIGN AFFAIRS

MINUTES OF SUBCOMMITTEE ON *Africa, Global Health, Global Human Rights, and International Organizations* HEARING

Day __*Wednesday*__ Date __*March 18, 2015*__ Room __*2255 Rayburn HOB*__

Starting Time __*10:21 a.m.*__ Ending Time __*12:07 p.m.*__

Recesses [__*0*__] (___ to ___) (___ to ___) (___ to ___) (___ to ___) (___ to ___) (___ to ___)

Presiding Member(s)

Rep. Tom Emmer, Rep. Curt Clawson

Check all of the following that apply:

Open Session ☑   Electronically Recorded (taped) ☑
Executive (closed) Session ☐   Stenographic Record ☑
Televised ☑

TITLE OF HEARING:

U.S. Election Support in Africa

SUBCOMMITTEE MEMBERS PRESENT:

Rep. Mark Meadows, Rep. Karen Bass, Rep. Ami Bera

NON-SUBCOMMITTEE MEMBERS PRESENT: *(Mark with an * if they are not members of full committee.)*

HEARING WITNESSES: Same as meeting notice attached? Yes ☑ No ☐
(If "no", please list below and include title, agency, department, or organization.)

STATEMENTS FOR THE RECORD: *(List any statements submitted for the record.)*

Statement of Rep. Chris Smith, submitted by Rep. Chris Smith
Response from Mr. Postel of USAID to question posed by Mr. Emmer
Response from Mr. Postel of USAID to question posed by Ms. Bass
Response from Mr. Postel of USAID to question posed by Mr. Meadows

TIME SCHEDULED TO RECONVENE _____
or
TIME ADJOURNED __*12:07 p.m.*__

_____
Subcommittee Staff Director

Statement of Rep. Chris Smith
"U.S. Election Support in Africa"
Subcommittee on Africa, Global Health, Global Human Rights, and International
Organizations
March 18, 2015

There is widespread, bipartisan agreement that the spread of constitutional democracy and representative government is a substantive good.

While it is easy to applaud democracy in the abstract, however, people often tend to ignore the procedural mechanisms that need to be in place that make elected government possible. It is this issue – the ignored "guts" and "gizzards" of elections – that is the topic of our hearing today.

For years, many non-governmental organizations providing electoral support have felt that U.S. funding for the electoral processes in Africa did not match the need for technical assistance to election commissions, political parties, and civil society voter education, not to mention providing election observers to make sure elections are fair. In some cases, funding is too limited; in other cases, it is provided too late to monitor the entire electoral process comprehensively.

Here in the United States, we have over the years experienced various irregularities in our elections. However, we have a watchful media and civil society, as well as a functional court system to address problems that occur. That does not prevent all injustices from taking place, but it does ensure that the kind of rampant injustice that divides societies and leads to violence will not completely discredit the democratic process in this country.

Unfortunately, that is not the case for some countries in Africa, and the failure of democratic processes can have deadly results. A troubled Angolan election in 1992 led to resumption of civil war. Post-election violence erupted in Kenya in 2007 due to questionable results in the balloting. A similar issue with the 2010 election in Cote d'Ivoire led to armed conflict and competing claims to power in that country, with both contenders claiming to be president. We hope that such an outcome won't take place in Nigerian elections scheduled for later this month. We recall that in the aftermath of the 2011 Nigerian elections, more than 1,000 people were killed and more than 700 houses of worship were destroyed. Ethnic and religious resentments linger to this day in Nigeria.

In too many places in Africa, election manipulation is so pervasive and so comprehensive that the thought of a free and fair election in Ethiopia, Sudan and Zimbabwe is considered beyond the realm of possibility.

Since the wave of multi-party elections in Africa in the 1990s, the U.S. government has devoted billions of dollars in assisting democratic election processes in Africa. In some cases, this electoral assistance has been well-designed and successful, but in other cases, it has been hurried and ineffective.

There appear to be two main reasons for these inconsistent outcomes. First, the government-wide need for austerity has compressed budgets for many programs, and democracy and governance has been considered a prime target for budget trimming. I believe this has been a short-sighted practice since it has led to violence, unrest and instability that has cost much more to address than it would had there been an appropriate response to the election process in the first place.

Second, there seems to be a lack of commitment to properly addressing deficiencies in the electoral processes in some countries. U.S. Agency for International Development training materials suggest that there is a realization of the entirety of an election process. The U.S. assistance program in Kenya in advance of the 2014 elections was an example of an imaginative and comprehensive election assistance program, but the same cannot be said for U.S. assistance in other elections in Africa.

Too often, insufficient attention is paid to efforts to change constitutions in ways that affect election outcomes. For example, when the constitution changed the victory threshold and eliminated a second round in the Democratic Republic of the Congo elections in 2011, not much was made of this development. Having a plurality allowed an unpopular government to retain power when a second round might have produced a different outcome and more vote satisfaction.

It is not enough to suggest a government of national unity in the face of a questionable election. I believe this practice is the result of a misinterpretation of what that has meant in the United States. It is true that the winning U.S. presidential candidate here has traditionally included at least one member of the opposition party in his cabinet, but it is never the candidate against whom the winning candidate ran in the elections. It is illogical to assume that the president would provide an opportunity for his opponent to build his credentials for a possible future run for office, and it is equally illogical to assume that this opposition leader would take actions to bring credit to his likely opponent in the next election. At best, there is a situation in which there are cross-purposes leading to thwarted governance. At worst, it can lead to chaos within government.

Yet this is what we urge African governments to do, and this strategy has failed to one extent or another in Kenya, Zimbabwe and South Africa. Yet this practice seems not to have been seriously questioned but apparently continues to be a policy option in the case of botched elections in Africa – a doubling down where a wrong-headed policy needs to be jettisoned! The international community appears poised to recommend this strategy once again in South Sudan, a country we help create but one which since then has been treated with indifference bordering on malpractice.

Today's hearing is thus intended to examine not only the budget for democracy and governance, especially as it involves election assistance, but also the strategies used in determining which elections will receive the appropriate investment of time and resources.

Our hearing is just a step in ensuring that our government helps to prevent problems before they occur and become larger crises. In doing so, we not only hope to guarantee the proper functioning of the democratic process in African countries, but also save lives and institutions unnecessarily lost or destroyed in post-election violence.